» CONTENT

Chapter 1
OVERVIEW

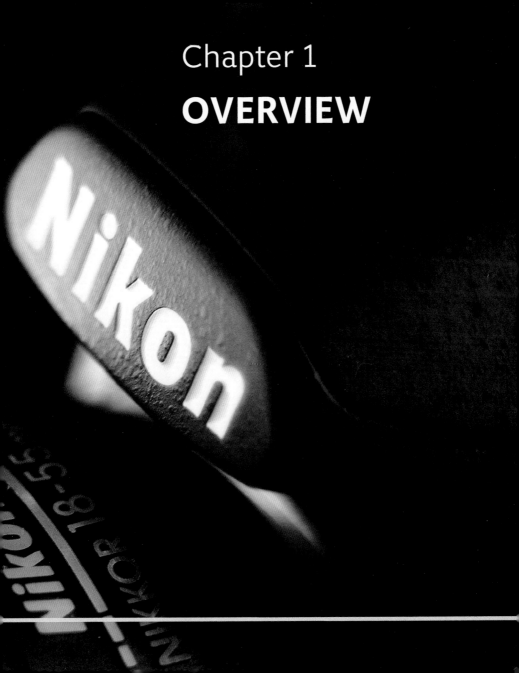

1 OVERVIEW

The D3100 is Nikon's new entry-level digital single-lens reflex camera (DSLR). Like its predecessors in this bracket, it marries the versatility and image quality of an SLR with the simplicity and ease of handling of the best digital compacts. It advances beyond its predecessors in several ways, notably by adding Live View and HD movie shooting. In fact it is the first Nikon DSLR, if only by a few weeks, to offer Full HD movie quality.

The D3100 has a straightforward look, with fewer buttons and dials than many other Nikon DSLRs. Its Guide Menu, in particular, is designed to lead new users through the picture-taking process in a straightforward way. However, the D3100 boasts many of the features of more advanced and even professional cameras, including highly controllable exposure modes such as Aperture Priority, Shutter Priority, and Manual.

The D3100's compact size, light weight, and uncluttered appearance will make it attractive to new DSLR users, but there's still a powerful camera behind that simple interface. Most importantly, the image quality is excellent and—when the camera is used appropriately—meets very demanding standards. It allows, and even invites, the user to explore the wide range of possibilities that lie beyond the basic Guide and Auto settings, encouraging a smooth progression into more creative approaches to photography.

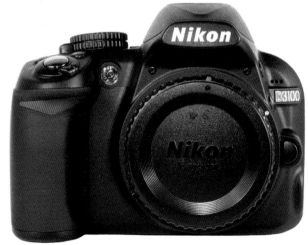

NIKON D3100 »
D3100 front view.

» NIKON DSLR HISTORY

Nikon has always valued continuity as well as innovation. When the major manufacturers introduced their first viable autofocus 35mm cameras in the 1980s, most of them ditched their existing lens mounts, but Nikon stayed true to its tried and tested F-mount system. This means it is still possible to use many classic Nikon lenses, even with the latest digital cameras such as the D3100, although some camera functions may be lost—autofocus being the most obvious.

Nikon's first DSLR was the E2s, with a 1.3 megapixel sensor. It had no rear screen, and images could only be viewed by connecting it to an external device, so the direct line of descent of the D3100 begins with the 2.7 megapixel D1, introduced in 1999. The D1 is one of the most influential digital cameras ever produced, and the first DSLR to match the flexibility and ease of handling of 35mm SLRs. Its sensor adopted the DX format *(see page 11)*, which was subsequently used in every Nikon DSLR until the arrival of the "full-frame" D3 with its FX format sensor.

In 2004, Nikon introduced their first "enthusiast" DSLR—the 6-megapixel D70—with the D50 arriving the following year. While the D50 was essentially a simplified D70, the D40, launched in 2006, was designed from scratch for ease of use. Its control interface centered on the rear LCD screen, with no separate control panel, and used a single command dial where previous models had two. The D60 (2008) added a higher resolution sensor, but otherwise closely resembled the D40.

Toward the end of 2008, Nikon released the D90, which was awash with new features, including Live View, dust removal, improved low-light performance, and a headline-grabbing movie mode. Many of these were replicated in the 2009 release of the D5000, which also boasted an articulating rear screen.

A few months later, the D3000 appeared and, despite the jump from a two-digit to four-digit model number, it was clearly a direct descendant of the D40 and D60. Although it was also influenced by the more recent D5000, the D3000 lacked a folding screen, had no Live View, and could not shoot movies—but it did introduce Nikon users to the new Guide Mode.

The D3000 has now evolved into the D3100, and while the latest model closely resembles its predecessor in many ways, there is no doubt that it is a significantly different camera, adding Live View and HD movie recording, not to mention a new 14.2-megapixel CMOS sensor.

1999: Nikon D1

The D1 was that rare thing—a truly revolutionary camera that made digital photography a practical, everyday proposition for thousands of professionals, not to mention a good number of amateur "early adopters."

2004: Nikon D70

Nikon scored a huge hit with the D70, a camera that persuaded a host of enthusiasts and many professionals (including the author of this book) to move away from film and take their first step into the world of digital photography.

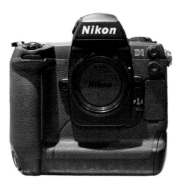

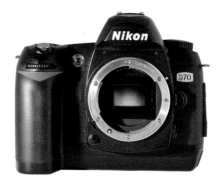

2006: Nikon D40

The 6-megapixel D40 was Nikon's first true entry-level DSLR, combining a compact, light, sturdy body, with a new interface that was both highly accessible and intuitive.

2009: Nikon D3000

The D3000 had much in common with the D40 and D60, but its headline feature was its innovative Guide Mode, designed specifically to help newcomers get to grips with both photography and digital technology.

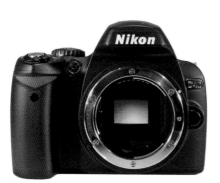

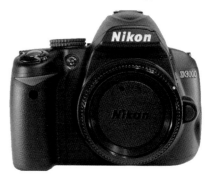

» NIKON DX FORMAT SENSORS

Nikon's DX format sensor, measuring approximately 23.6 x 15.8mm, was used in every Nikon DSLR from the D1 (1999) right through to the arrival of the full-frame D3 in 2007, and it continues to be used in the majority of DSLR cameras in Nikon's range.

The format dictates a 1.5x magnification factor, relative to the same lenses used on 35mm cameras, which is a factor that has been consistent since the launch of the D1. However, there have been changes in this time, not least the number of pixels that have been squeezed onto the sensor, which has risen from the D1's now modest 2.7 million to 14.2 million pixels in the D3100 (and 16.2 million in the D7000).

With 14.2 million effective pixels, the D3100 produces images at a native size of 4608 x 3072 pixels, which is more than enough for most purposes, and suitable for both large prints, and book and magazine reproduction. Unlike many of its predecessors, the D3100 uses a CMOS (Complementary Metal Oxide Semiconductor) sensor, rather than a CCD (Charge-coupled Device), which means that CCD sensors no longer feature on any current Nikon DSLR.

› About the Nikon D3100

From the front, the Nikon D3100 is almost identical to the D3000, but on the rear it gains a Live View/movie switch and an additional control button alongside its 3-inch LCD screen. Internally, major features include the 14.2-megapixel CMOS sensor with self-cleaning function, EXPEED 2 image-processing, and a maximum shooting rate of 3 frames per second.

Like all Nikon SLRs, the D3100 is part of a vast system of lenses, accessories, and software, and this expanded guide will walk you through all aspects of the camera's operation, as well as examining its relationship to the Nikon camera system as a whole.

1 » MAIN FEATURES OF THE NIKON D3100

Sensor
14.2 effective megapixel, DX format, RGB, CMOS sensor measuring 23.6 x 15.8mm and capable of producing a maximum image size of 4608 x 3072 pixels. Includes a self-cleaning function.

Image processor
Uses Nikon's EXPEED 2 image-processing system, which features 12-bit analog-to-digital (A/D) conversion.

Focus
11-Point autofocus system, supported by Nikon Scene Recognition System, which tracks subjects by shape, position, and color. Three focus modes: Single-servo AF (AF-S), Continuous-servo AF (AF-C), and Manual (M) focus. Auto-selection autofocus (AF-A) automatically selects from AF-S and AF-C. Four AF-area modes: Single-point AF, Dynamic-area AF, 3D tracking AF, and Auto-area AF. Rapid focus-point selection and focus lock.

Exposure
Three metering modes: matrix, center-weighted, and spot metering. 3D Color Matrix Metering II uses a 420-pixel color sensor to analyze data based on brightness, color, contrast, and subject distance from all areas of the frame. With non-G/D-type lenses, Standard Color Matrix Metering II is employed.

Two full auto modes: Auto and Auto (flash off). Four user-controlled modes: Programmed auto with flexible program (P), Aperture Priority auto (A), Shutter Priority auto (S), and Manual (M). Six Scene Modes: Portrait, Landscape, Child, Sports, Close-up, and Night portrait. Guide Mode uses menu screens to guide users to the appropriate Scene Mode. ISO range from ISO 100–ISO 3200, extendable to ISO 6400 (Hi1) or ISO 12800 (Hi2). Exposure compensation covers ±5EV.

Shutter
Shutter speeds from 1/4000 sec. to 30 seconds, plus B (Bulb). Maximum frame advance 3 fps (frames per second).

Viewfinder
Pentamirror viewfinder with 95% coverage and 0.8x magnification.

Buffer
Buffer capacity allows up to 30 JPEG frames to be captured in a continuous burst at 3fps, or nine RAW files (rate slows to approximately 1fps).

Built-in flash
Pop-up flash (manually activated) with Guide Number of 12m or 39ft at ISO 100. Supports i-TTL balanced fill-flash for DSLR when matrix or centerweighted metering

is selected, and Standard i-TTL flash for DSLR when spot metering is selected. Up to eight flash-sync modes (dependent on exposure mode in use): fill-flash, front-curtain sync, slow sync, rear-curtain sync, red-eye reduction, auto slow sync, and slow sync with red-eye reduction. Flash compensation from -3EV to +1EV.

LCD monitor
Fixed 3-inch, 230,000-dot TFT LCD display with 100% frame coverage.

File formats
12-bit NEF (RAW) and 8-bit JPEG (Fine/Normal/Basic).

System back-up
Compatible with more than 60 current Nikkor lenses and many non-current lenses (functionality varies with older lenses), SB-series flashguns, Wireless Remote Control ML-L3, GP-1 GPS unit, and many more Nikon system accessories.

Software
Supplied with *Nikon Transfer* and *Nikon View NX2.* Compatible with *Nikon Capture NX2* and many third-party imaging applications.

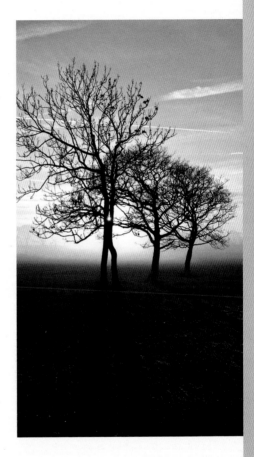

1 » FULL FEATURES AND CAMERA LAYOUT

FRONT OF CAMERA

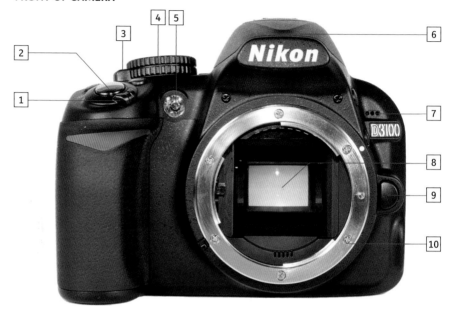

FRONT OF CAMERA

1	Power switch	6	Built-in flash
2	Shutter-release button	7	Microphone
3	Release-mode selector	8	Mirror
4	Mode dial	9	Lens-release button
5	AF-assist illuminator/Self-timer lamp/Red-eye reduction lamp	10	Lens mount

BACK OF CAMERA

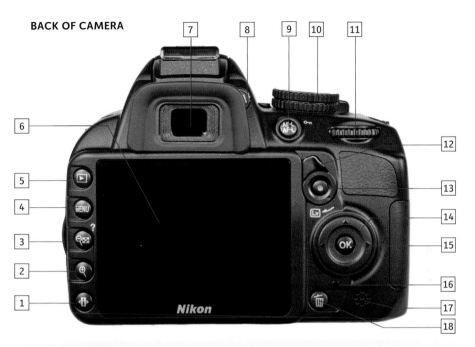

BACK OF CAMERA

1	Information edit button	10	Mode dial
2	Playback zoom-in button	11	Command dial
3	Playback zoom-out/Thumbnail button	12	Live View switch
4	Menu button	13	Movie record button
5	Playback button	14	Multi-selector
6	LCD monitor	15	OK button
7	Viewfinder eyepiece	16	Memory card access lamp
8	Diopter adjustment dial	17	Speaker
9	AE-L/AF-L/Protect button	18	Delete button

1 » FULL FEATURES AND CAMERA LAYOUT

TOP OF CAMERA   LEFT SIDE

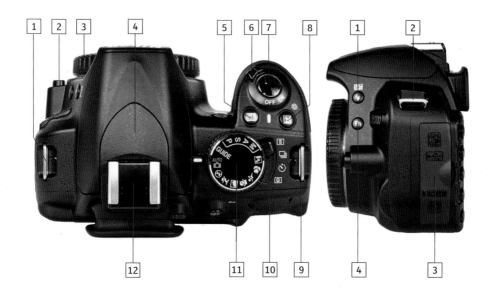

TOP OF CAMERA

1	Camera strap eyelet	10	Release-mode selector
2	Lens-release button	11	Mode dial
3	Body cap	12	Accessory shoe
4	Built-in flash		
5	Information button	**LEFT SIDE**	
6	Power switch	1	Flash mode button
7	Shutter-release button	2	Camera strap eyelet
8	Exposure compensation button	3	Connector cover
9	Camera strap eyelet	4	Function button

RIGHT SIDE

BOTTOM OF CAMERA

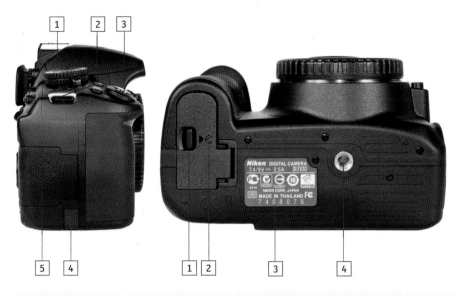

RIGHT SIDE

1	Mode dial
2	Camera strap eyelet
3	Shutter-release button
4	DC cord hole
5	Memory card slot cover

BOTTOM OF CAMERA

1	Battery compartment release
2	Battery compartment
3	Camera serial number
4	Tripod socket (¼in.)

» VIEWFINDER DISPLAY

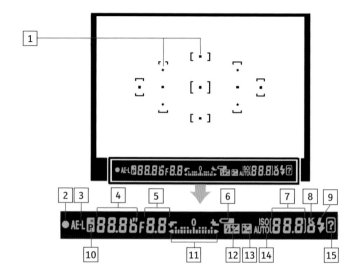

1	Focus points	8	"K" (appears when memory remains for over 1000 frames)
2	Focus indicator	9	Flash ready indicator
3	Autoexposure (AE) lock indicator	10	Flexible program indicator
4	Shutter speed	11	Exposure indicator
5	Aperture (f-number)		Exposure compensation display
6	Battery indicator		Electronic rangefinder
7	Number of exposures remaining	12	Flash compensation indicator
	Number of shots remaining before memory buffer fills White balance recording indicator Exposure compensation value Flash compensation value ISO sensitivity value	13	Exposure compensation indicator
		14	Auto ISO sensitivity indicator
		15	Warning indicator

» LCD SCREEN

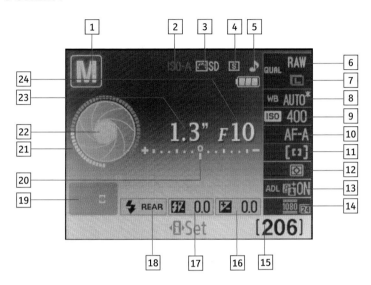

1	Shooting mode	12	Metering
2	Auto ISO indicator	13	Active D-Lighting
3	Picture Control	14	Movie frame size
4	Release mode	15	Number of exposures remaining
5	"Beep" indicator	16	Exposure compensation
6	Image quality	17	Flash compensation
7	Image size	18	Flash mode
8	White balance	19	Auto-area AF indicator
9	ISO sensitivity		3D-tracking indicator
10	Focus mode		Focus point
11	AF-area mode		

20	Exposure indicator
	Exposure compensation
	Electronic rangefinder
21	Shutter speed display
22	Aperture display
23	Shutter speed
24	Aperture

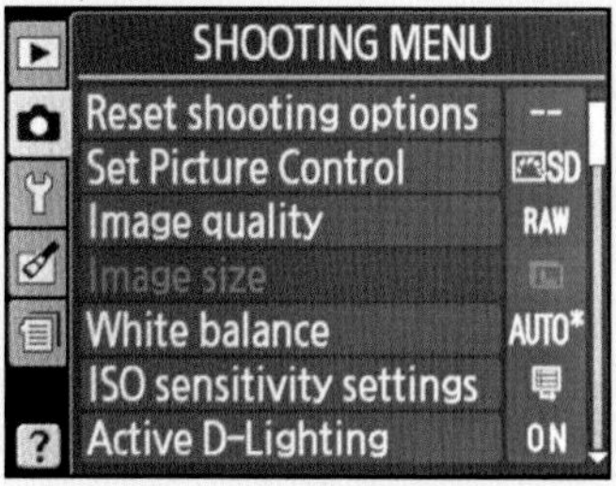

1 » MENU DISPLAYS

```
        SHOOTING MENU
▶
⌂   Reset shooting options    --
    Set Picture Control      ⊠SD
    Image quality            RAW
⌀   Image size               ⊡
    White balance            AUTO*
    ISO sensitivity settings ⊡
?   Active D-Lighting        ON
```

Shooting menu
> Reset shooting options
> Set Picture Control
> Image quality
> Image size
> White balance
> ISO sensitivity settings
> Active D-Lighting
> Auto distortion control
> Color space
> Noise reduction
> AF-area mode
> AF-assist
> Metering
> Movie settings
> Built-in flash

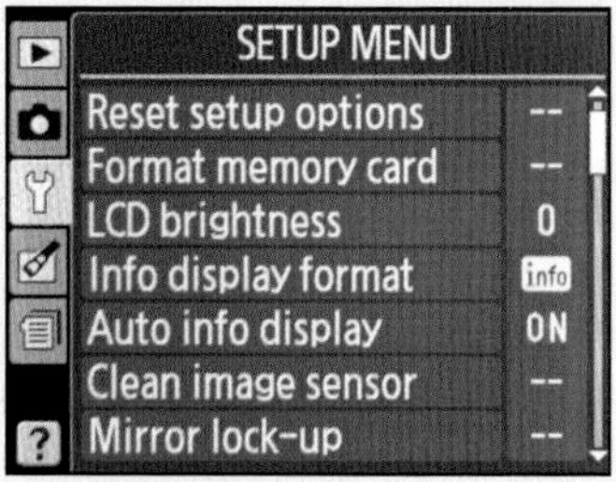

```
        SETUP MENU
▶
⌂   Reset setup options      --
    Format memory card       --
⌀   LCD brightness           0
    Info display format      info
    Auto info display        ON
    Clean image sensor       --
?   Mirror lock-up           --
```

Setup Menu
> Reset setup options
> Format memory card
> LCD brightness
> Info display format
> Auto info display
> Clean image sensor
> Mirror lock-up
> Video mode
> HDMI
> Flicker reduction
> Time zone and date
> Language
> Image comment
> Auto image rotation
> Dust Off ref photo
> Auto off timers
> Self-timer delay
> Beep
> Rangefinder
> File number sequence
> Buttons
> Slot empty release lock
> Date imprint
> Storage folder
> GPS
> Firmware version

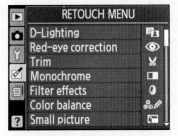

Retouch Menu

> D-Lighting
> Red-eye correction
> Trim
> Monochrome
> Filter effects
> Color balance
> Small picture
> Image overlay
> NEF (RAW) processing
> Quick retouch
> Straighten
> Distortion control
> Fisheye
> Color outline
> Perspective control
> Miniature effect
> Edit movie

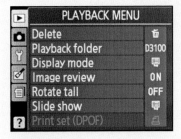

Playback Menu

> Delete
> Playback folder
> Display mode
> Image review
> Rotate tall
> Slide show
> Print set (DPOF)

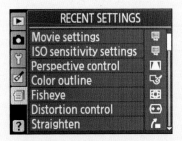

Recent Settings

> Displays recently used settings

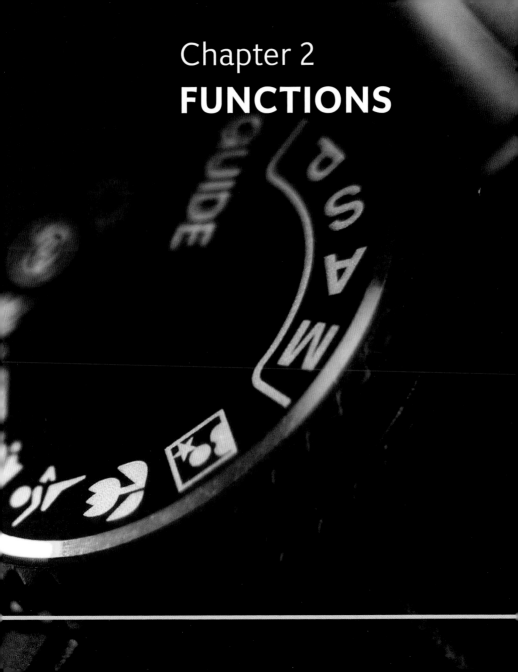

Chapter 2
FUNCTIONS

2 FUNCTIONS

For all its promises of simplicity, the Nikon D3100 still sports over a dozen control buttons, a Mode Dial, a Command Dial, and a multi-selector. It may well appear complex and daunting to users familiar with digital compacts or 35mm SLRs, but the D3100 is genuinely and thoughtfully designed to be as simple to use as any "point-and-shoot" camera.

It should be ready for use when you first unpack it, and at any time you can quickly reset it to full auto operation: to be sure that all settings are restored to their original defaults use **Reset shooting options** in the Shooting Menu. (For a complete reset also use the Reset option in the Setup menu).

However, the D3100 offers far greater flexibility than the average point-and-shoot camera, not to mention superior image quality. Its intelligent design allows users to make a straightforward, progressive transition from leaving everything to the camera to taking full control of its many functions.

Leaving the camera at its default settings misses out on much of its imaging power, and the intention of this chapter is to provide a step-by-step introduction to its most important features and functions. Even in a much longer book it would be impossible to fully explore every detail, so we will concentrate on those aspects relevant to the majority of photographers.

Nikon's evolutionary approach to camera design means the D3100 will feel familiar to anyone used to previous Nikon DSLRs (especially the D40(x), D60, or D3000), but it would be a mistake to start using the D3100 in the same way as earlier models, without exploring its new features.

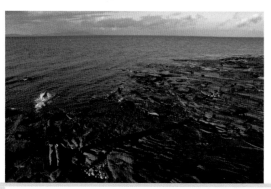

UNLIMITED OPTIONS «
When you unpack a new camera, it's tempting to start shooting right away. Although taking pictures is the best way to learn, it still makes sense to peruse this book first, to make sure that you don't miss out on new features and functions.

ISO: 200 *Focal Length:* 24mm
Shutter Speed: 1/125 sec.
Aperture: f/10

» CAMERA PREPARATION

Some basic operations, such as charging the battery and inserting a memory card, are essential before the camera can be used. These operations, and others such as changing lenses, may seem trivial, but it's important to be able to perform them quickly and smoothly in awkward situations or when time is short.

Setting the time, date, and time zone is also a good idea.

› Attaching the strap

To attach the supplied strap, make sure that the padded side will face inward (so the

THE STRAP   ⌄
The strap is shown threaded but not yet tightened

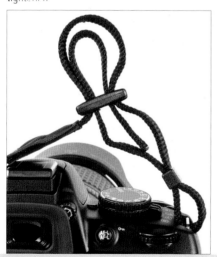

maker's name faces out). Attach either end to the appropriate eyelet, located at top left and right sides of the camera. Loosen the strap where it runs through the buckle, then pass the end of the strap through the eyelet and back through the buckle. Bring the end of the strap back through the buckle, under the first length of strap already threaded (see photo). Repeat the operation on the other side. Adjust the length as required, but make sure that a good length (minimum 2 inches/5cm) of strap extends beyond the buckle on each side to avoid any risk of it pulling through. When satisfied with the length, pull it firmly to seat it securely within the buckle.

> **Note:**
> This method is not the same as that shown in the Nikon *Quick Start Guide*, but is both more secure and neater.

› Adjusting the diopter

The D3100 offers dioptric adjustment between −1.7 and +0.5 m^{-1}, to allow for individual variations in eyesight; it's a good idea to optimize this for your eyesight (with glasses or contact lenses if you normally use them) before using the camera. The diopter adjustment control is immediately to the right of the viewfinder.

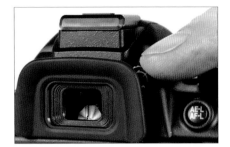

DIOPTER ADJUSTMENT ⌃

With the camera switched on, rotate the dial until the readouts and focus points marked in the viewfinder appear sharp. Unless your eyesight changes you only need to do this once. Supplementary viewfinder lenses are available if the built-in adjustment proves insufficient.

› Mounting lenses

Always switch the camera off before changing lenses. Start by removing the camera's body cap or, if there's a lens already mounted, press the lens release button and turn the lens clockwise (looking from the front of the camera) to remove it.

To mount a lens, remove the rear lens cap (if fitted) and align the index mark (white dot) on the lens with the corresponding mark on the camera body. Insert the lens gently into the camera and turn it counterclockwise until it clicks home. Do not use force—if the lens is

correctly aligned it will mount smoothly.

Most Nikon F-mount lenses can be used safely on the Nikon D3100, although many functions are lost with older lenses and autofocus is only available with AF-I and AF-S lenses. With older lenses with an aperture ring, rotate this to the minimum aperture (f/22, for example) before using it.

MOUNTING LENSES ⌄

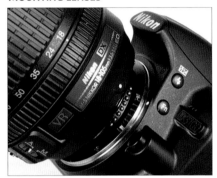

Caution

Take care when changing lenses, as dropping either the lens or the camera is definitely to be avoided! Take extra care in dusty environments and beware of wind that could introduce dust or sand while the camera's interior is exposed. Avoid touching the electrical contacts on the lens and camera body, as dirty contacts can cause a malfunction, and replace the lens or body cap as soon as possible.

› Inserting and removing memory cards

The D3100 stores images on Secure Digital (SD) cards, including high-capacity SDHC and SDXC cards. To remove or insert a memory card:

1) Switch the camera **OFF** and check that the green access lamp on the back of the camera is not lit.

2) Slide the card slot cover on the right side of the camera toward the rear. It will spring open.

3) To remove a memory card, press the card gently into the slot and it will spring out slightly. Remove the card fully.

4) Insert a card with its label side toward you and the rows of terminals along the card edge facing into the slot. The "cut-off" corner of the card will be at top left as you look at it from the back of the camera. Push the memory card into the slot until it clicks home. The green access lamp will light briefly.

5) Close the card slot cover.

INSERTING A MEMORY CARD »

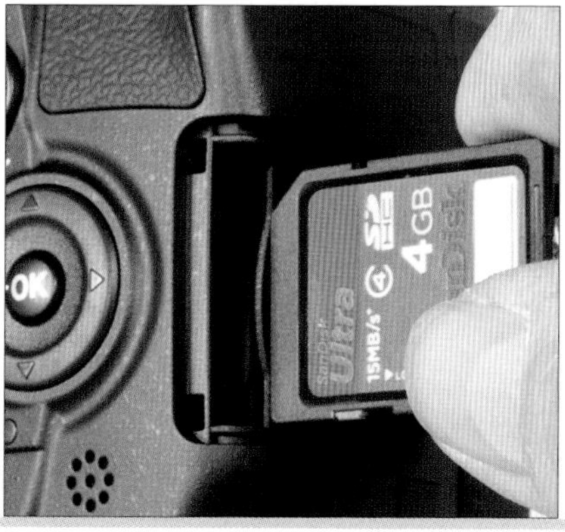

Warning!

Inserting a memory card incorrectly may damage the camera.

When the access lamp is lit or blinking do not open the card slot cover or remove the battery.

› Formatting a memory card

It is recommended that you format a new memory card (or one that has been used in another camera) before using it with the D3100. Formatting is also the quickest way to erase existing images on the card, and therefore requires caution—make sure any images have been downloaded before you format a memory card.

To format a memory card

1) Press **MENU** and then select the Setup menu 🔧 from the symbols at left of the screen.

2) Select **Format memory card** and then press (OK).

3) Select **Yes** when prompted, then (OK).

› Inserting the battery

The Nikon D3100 is supplied with an EN-EL14 lithium-ion rechargeable battery. The battery should be fully charged before first use (see *Battery charging*).

Turn the camera upside down and locate the battery compartment below the hand-grip. Release the latch to open the compartment and insert the battery, contacts first, with the maker's name facing away from the camera. Press the battery gently down and then shut the battery compartment cover until it clicks home.

To remove the battery, make sure the camera is switched **OFF**, and open the

Warning!

Always switch the camera off before removing or replacing the battery.

compartment cover as above. Turn the camera right-way up and the battery should slip out a small way. Pull it gently the rest of the way.

› Battery charging

Only use the supplied MH-24 Charger to charge the battery, as other chargers could damage it. Remove the terminal cover (if present) from the battery and insert the battery into the charger with the maker's name uppermost and the terminals facing the contacts on the charger. Press the battery gently, but firmly, into position and plug the charger into a mains outlet. The Charge lamp will blink while the battery is charging, then shine steadily when charging is complete. A completely discharged battery will take around 90 minutes to recharge fully.

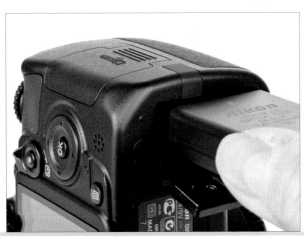

«
INSERTING THE BATTERY

› Battery life

Various factors determine how long the battery can last before it needs recharging. Working temperature can be critical and Nikon do not recommend use at temperatures below 32°F (0°C) or above 104°F (40°C). Other factors that can reduce battery life include heavy use of the LCD screen (reviewing every image you shoot, for example), extended use of the built-in flash, and protracted use of Live View/movie shooting.

Under standard test conditions by CIPA, the D3100 delivers approximately 550 shots from a fully charged EN-EL14 battery, although careful use can double this figure, and heavy use will reduce it. The Information Display and viewfinder give an approximate indication of how much charge remains, and these icons blink when the battery is nearly exhausted. For information on alternative power sources, see *Chapter 8*.

› Switching the camera on

The power switch, surrounding the shutter-release button, has two settings:

OFF The camera will not operate.
ON The camera operates normally.

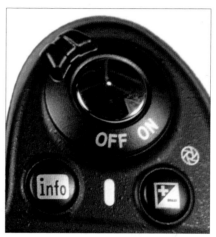

POWER SWITCH AND SHUTTER-RELEASE BUTTON

Tips

The battery charger can be used abroad (100–240 v AC 50/60 Hz) with a commercially available plug-adapter.

Do not attach a voltage transformer to the battery charger as this may damage it.

Tip

*If the power switch is turned **OFF** while the camera is recording image file(s) to the memory card, the camera will finish the process before turning off.*

2 » BASIC CAMERA FUNCTIONS

With the strap, lens, battery, and memory card on board, the camera is ready to shoot and, initially, it will be set to its basic Auto mode when you first turn it on. In beginning to explore a wider range of options, the key controls at this stage are the shutter-release button, Mode Dial, Command Dial, and multi-selector, along with the release-mode selector.

Settings that are affected by these controls are seen in the Information Display on the rear LCD screen, and some are also displayed through the viewfinder. However, in the Full Auto and Scene Modes it is perfectly possible (although not necessarily recommended!) to shoot without reference to any of these displays or controls.

› Operating the shutter

The shutter-release button operates in two stages. Pressing it lightly, until initial resistance is felt, activates the metering and focus functions. If you maintain this half-pressure on the button, focus is locked in Single-servo AF.

Half-pressure also clears the Information Display, menus, or image playback, making the D3100 ready to shoot. Press the button more firmly (but still smoothly) to take the picture.

› The Mode Dial

The Mode Dial is probably the first port of call when it comes to changing key camera setting and simply rotates so you can set it to the desired position. There are 13 possible positions, which we can divide

THE MODE DIAL   ❯❯
Mode Dial and release-mode selector

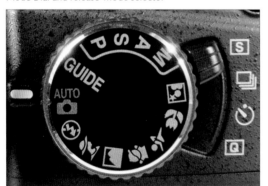

Warning!

The Mode Dial does not have a lock, so check to make sure it is set correctly, as accidental shifts into a different mode can occur.

into four groups: Full Auto, User-control modes, Scene Modes, and Guide Mode. For more detail on these, see Exposure Modes (*pages 35–37*) and Guide Mode (*pages 35 and 77–83*).

› The Command Dial

The Command Dial falls naturally under the right thumb when the camera is in the shooting position.

Operating the Command Dial

The Command Dial is fundamental to the operation of the Nikon D3100, especially in the User-control modes. Its function is flexible, varying according to the operating mode at the time: In Shutter Priority (**S**) or Manual (**M**) mode, rotating the command dial selects the shutter speed, while in

Aperture Priority (**A**) mode it selects the aperture. In Program (**P**) it engages flexible program, changing the shutter speed and aperture combination. When shooting in Full Auto or the Scene Modes, the Command Dial on its own has no effect.

› The Multi-selector

As well as the command dial, the other principal control point on the D3100 is the multi-selector. Its main use when taking photographs is to select and change settings in the Information Display. The (OK) button at its center is used to confirm settings. The multi-selector is also used for navigating through the menus, and through images on playback. Its operation is similar to the control system of many mobile phones and other devices.

THE COMMAND DIAL �

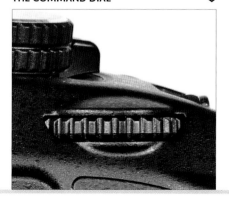

THE MULTI-SELECTOR ✳

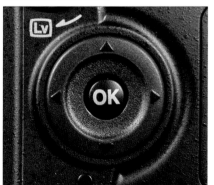

2 » THE INFORMATION DISPLAY

The Information Display is central to using the Nikon D3100. If you are familiar with traditional camera controls, then using buttons and dials may seem a little strange at first, although it soon proves to be a straightforward (if slightly slower) way of accessing camera functions.

To activate the Information Display, use any one of these three methods:

Half-press and release the shutter-release button *(if you maintain pressure the Information Display will not appear)*

Press the info **button on the top of the camera**

Press the ◄i► button on the rear of the camera

Each of these will bring up a display showing the selected exposure mode, the aperture and shutter speed, and a range of other information. This screen can be displayed in a choice of two formats—**Graphic** or **Classic**. **Graphic**, which is active by default, uses icons and pictures to illustrate the effect of various settings, while the **Classic** format presents the information in a more traditional, mostly numerical, way. The color scheme can be changed for both of these display formats, with the options exercised through the Setup menu.

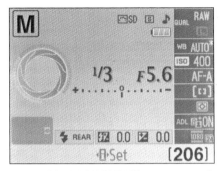

THE INFORMATION DISPLAY ☆
(GRAPHIC FORMAT)

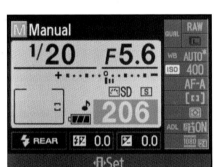

THE INFORMATION DISPLAY ☆
(CLASSIC FORMAT)

› Screen orientation

When using the Information Display, the camera detects whether it is being held in landscape or portrait orientation and sets the display accordingly.

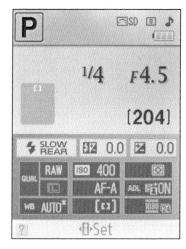

THE INFORMATION DISPLAY IN PORTRAIT ORIENTATION ≈

› The Active Information Display

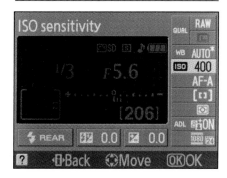

The initial Active Information Display is passive, in that it displays many settings but does not allow them to be changed. To make changes, press ◄🖩► while the initial display is visible (if the screen is blank, press the button twice). The screen changes and the multi-selector can now be used to move quickly through the various settings. To make changes, press (OK), and the range of options for that setting will appear. Use the multi-selector to scroll through the options and, when the one you want is highlighted, press (OK) again to select it.

> **Note:**
> The term "Active Information Display" is used for this screen throughout this guide, although it is not used in Nikon's manual for the D3100.

2 » RELEASE MODES

"Release mode" may seem a slightly obscure term, but it determines whether the camera takes a single picture or shoots continuously, and can also allow the shot to be delayed. The release mode is chosen using the Release Mode selector, which is below and right of the Mode Dial, with four release modes available.

RELEASE MODE OPTIONS	
Setting	Description
[S] Single Frame	The camera takes a single shot each time the shutter release is fully depressed.
Continuous	The camera fires continuously as long as the shutter release is fully depressed. The maximum frame rate is 3 frames per second (fps).
Self-timer	The shutter is released a predetermined time after the shutter-release button is fully depressed. Can be used to minimize camera shake and for self-portraits. The default interval is 10 seconds, but this can be changed to 2 seconds through the Shooting menu.
[Q] Quiet shutter release	As Single Frame, but there are no alert beeps and the mirror-return after each shot is damped to provide a quieter release.

› The buffer

Before they are written to the memory card, images are stored in the camera's internal memory, or "buffer." The maximum number of images that can be recorded in a continuous burst depends upon file quality, release mode, memory card capacity, and how much buffer space is available. The figure for the number of burst frames possible at current settings is shown in the viewfinder at bottom right when the shutter-release button is half depressed, for example **r05** would be displayed if the camera could record a burst of five frames.

If **0** appears, the buffer is full. No more shots can be taken until enough data has been transferred to the memory card to free up space in the buffer. This normally happens very quickly, although you may need to release pressure on the shutter-release button momentarily before shooting will resume.

» EXPOSURE MODES

The choice of exposure mode makes a significant difference to the amount of control the user can—or can't—exercise over the D3100. Exposure modes are selected using the Mode Dial on top of the camera and while the D3100 has a wide number of options, they can be conveniently divided into three main groups: Full Auto, Scene Modes, and User-control modes.

Guide Mode

Guide Mode is also selected on the Mode Dial, but is not in itself an exposure mode. Instead, it simply provides you with a guide that helps you choose from the other exposure modes.

In the Full Auto and Scene Modes the camera controls the majority of the camera settings. These go beyond basic shooting settings (such as shutter speed and aperture) to include options such as whether or not flash can be used. The choice of Scene mode also determines most aspects of how the camera processes the shot. The key difference between Full Auto and Scene Modes is that the Full Auto modes use general settings that aim to cover most eventualities while Scene Mode settings are tailored to particular shooting situations. User-control modes, by contrast, give the user complete freedom to control virtually everything on the camera.

MODE GROUP		EXPOSURE MODE	
Full Auto Modes	AUTO	Auto	Leave all decisions about
		Auto (flash off)	settings to the camera.
Scene Modes		Portrait	Choose the mode that best
		Landscape	suits the subject and
		Child	the camera then employs
		Sports	appropriate settings.
		Close up	
		Night portrait	
User-control Modes	**P**	Program	Allow much greater control
	S	Shutter Priority	over the full range of
	A	Aperture Priority	camera settings.
	M	Manual	

In its manual, Nikon calls these "Point and Shoot" modes, which is probably a fair reflection of the kind of photography for which they are likely to be used. In these modes the D3100 is capable of getting acceptable shots under most conditions, but the results may not always match what you had in mind. This is ideal for snapshots and when time is of the essence, but it limits creative control, and barely begins to exploit the camera's full potential.

There's only one difference between the two Full Auto modes. In **AUTO Auto mode** the built-in flash will pop up automatically when the camera determines light levels are too low. The flash can only be turned off via the Active Information Display unless a separate accessory flashgun is attached and switched on, in which case this overrides the built-in unit.

In **Auto (flash off)** mode the flash stays off and can't be activated manually. This is useful in situations where flash is banned or would be intrusive, or when you just want to discover what the D3100 can do in low light.

› Exposure warning

In all modes, if the camera detects that light levels are too low—or, more rarely, too high—for an acceptable exposure, a warning will be displayed in both the viewfinder and the Active Information Display. The viewfinder display blinks, and **Lo** or **Hi** appears in place of the shutter speed indication. In the Active Information

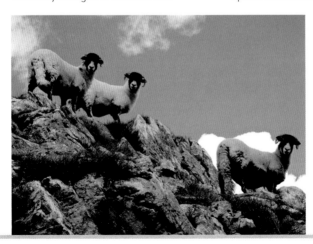

AUTO   **《**
Full Auto mode is ideal when shots need to be grabbed quickly.

ISO: 400
Focal Length: 65mm
Shutter Speed: 1/640 sec.
Aperture: f/10

Display you will see both a flashing question mark and a warning message such as "Subject is too dark": Pressing **?** brings up a more detailed message.

The camera will still take pictures under these conditions, but the results may be underexposed or subject to camera-shake if it's too dark, or overexposed if too bright.

The Nikon manual calls these "Creative Modes," a term calculated to irritate experienced photographers as they still take many decisions out of the photographer's hands. However, even the experienced may occasionally find them useful as a quick way to set the camera for shooting a particular kind of image.

Newcomers to DSLR photography will find Scene Modes are ideal for discovering the different ways in which the camera can interpret the same subject, making them a great stepping-stone to using the full range of exposure options offered by the D3100.

The first step is to understand how the various Scene Modes work and to be aware of the difference they can make to your images. Switching between Scene Modes doesn't just affect basic shooting parameters such as how the camera focuses and how it sets the shutter speed and aperture, they also determine how the image is processed by the camera (assuming you are shooting JPEG images). For instance, you can't choose which Nikon Picture Control will be applied, as these are predetermined. In 🏊 Portrait mode, for example, the camera applies a Portrait Picture Control that aims for natural (rather than excessively vivid) colors and is particularly kind to skin tones. All of the Scene Modes also employ **Auto White Balance**.

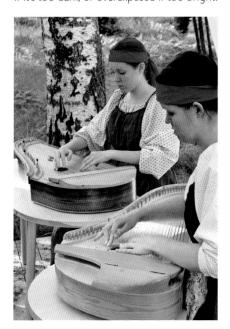

FLASH OFF ⌄
Auto (flash off) mode is suitable when flash is banned or would be disruptive.

ISO: 400 *Focal Length:* 50mm
Shutter Speed: 1/30 sec. *Aperture:* f/8

› Portrait

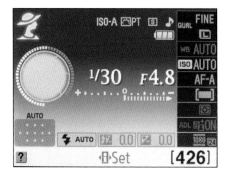

› Child

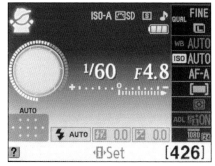

In Portrait mode the camera sets a relatively wide aperture to minimize the depth of field and help the subject stand out from the background. The camera also selects the focus point automatically, although you can switch to manual selection if you prefer. The flash automatically pops up if the camera determines that the light levels are too low, but can be turned off via the Active Information Display. Attaching a separate flash unit will automatically override the built-in flash, and usually improves the result dramatically.

Child mode is broadly similar to Portrait mode, but with one obvious difference: the camera tends to set faster shutter speeds. This is no doubt because children are less likely than adults to sit still when required. Colors are also handled slightly differently (using the Standard Picture Control, rather than the Portrait Picture Control) to produce results that are more vivid overall, but still give natural skin tones. The flash activates automatically, but can be turned off if preferred.

› Landscape

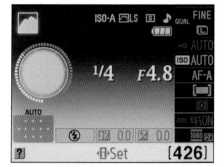

selects the central focus point, but allows you to change this selection using the multi-selector.

The Landscape Picture Control is applied to give vibrant colors and the built-in flash remains off, even in low light. There is no way to activate it manually, so if you would like some fill-in flash, you have to use a separate flash unit.

In Landscape mode, the camera sets a small aperture, aiming to maximize the depth of field. Small apertures mean that shutter speeds can be slow, so a tripod is often advisable. The camera initially

LANDSCAPE ❯❯

Landscape mode aims to keep both the foreground and background sharp.

ISO: 400 *Focal Length:* 18mm
Shutter Speed: 1/320 sec. *Aperture:* f/11

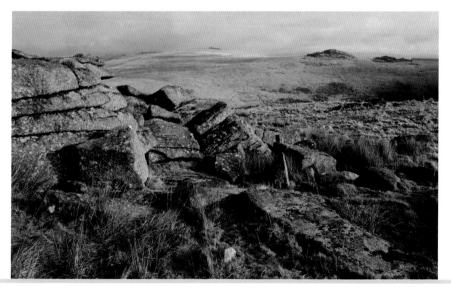

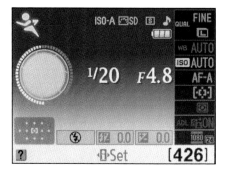

The flash remains off, even in low light, and there's no way to override this, so if you'd like a bit of fill-in flash you will have to use one of the User-control modes, or fit a separate flash. The Standard Picture Control is applied to produce natural-looking colors that are neither too muted, nor overly vibrant.

Sports mode is suitable for shooting not just sports, but other fast-moving subjects, including wildlife. The camera will try to set a fast shutter speed to freeze movement, which usually means a wide aperture is used, resulting in a shallow depth of field.

The D3100 initially selects the central focus point, but if it detects subject movement it will track it using the other ten focus points. You can also over-ride this initial selection yourself.

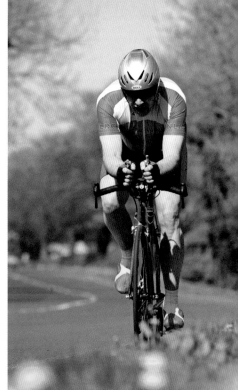

FREEZING MOVEMENT »
Sports mode aims to freeze the action.

ISO: 800 *Focal Length:* 300mm
Shutter Speed: 1/2000 sec. *Aperture:* f/8

› Close-up 🌷

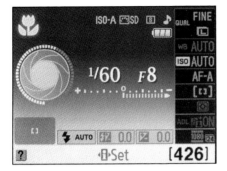

The built-in flash will activate automatically in low light, but it is worth noting that this is often far from ideal for close-up shots as the lens will often throw a shadow on the subject. It can be turned off via the Active Information Display if this is a problem. A better option is a separate accessory flash, which will automatically override the built-in unit.

As its name suggests, close-up mode is intended for shooting at close range. The camera sets a relatively small aperture to increase the depth of field and automatically selects the central focus point (although this can be overridden).

GETTING CLOSE ⬇
Close-up mode is versatile, but it's often best to turn the flash off.

ISO: 500 *Focal Length:* 300mm
Shutter Speed: 1/1200 sec. *Aperture:* f/7.1

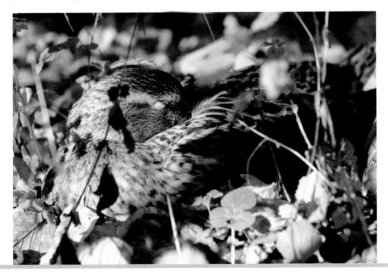

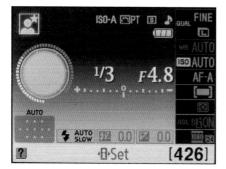
In most respects Night Portrait mode is similar to the regular Portrait mode, but when the ambient light is low it allows the camera to set a slow shutter speed to allow the background to register. For this reason, it is recommended that you use a tripod or other solid camera support. The built-in flash operates automatically, and while the results should be less harsh than using the regular Portrait mode at night, an accessory flash will improve matters. The flash can be turned off via the Active Information Display if preferred.

This mode would also be a reasonable choice for night-time landscapes, as well as portraits. However, the image is processed using the Portrait Picture Control to favor skin tones rather than give vivid images of city skylines. It is also worth noting that the maximum exposure time is 1 second; if a longer time is required, use Manual (**M**) mode.

NIGHT SHOTS ❯❯
Night Portrait mode can work well for evening landscapes, but it does not give vivid colors. Shooting RAW is the best way to overcome this.

ISO: 100 *Focal Length:* 38mm
Shutter Speed: 15 sec. *Aperture:* f/22

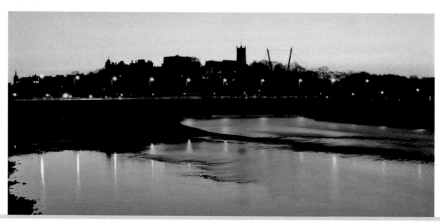

» USER-CONTROL MODES

Taking the picture

Basic picture taking is essentially the same in all **Full Auto** and **Scene** modes.

1) Select the desired mode by rotating the mode dial to the appropriate position.

2) Frame the picture.

3) Half-depress the release button to activate focusing and exposure. The focus point(s) will be displayed in the viewfinder image, and shutter speed and aperture settings will appear at the bottom of the viewfinder.

4) Fully depress the shutter release to take the picture.

The remaining four modes are traditional standards, which will be familiar to any experienced photographer. As well as allowing direct control over the basic settings of aperture and shutter speed (even in **P** mode through flexible program), these modes give full access to controls such as White Balance, Active D-Lighting, and Nikon Picture Controls. Between them, these modes give you absolute control over the look and feel of your images.

PROGRAMMED AUTO   ⩲

Programmed auto (or Program) mode allows users more scope to tailor the camera settings to suit their own creative ideas.

ISO: 200 *Focal Length:* 18mm
Shutter Speed: 1/13 sec. *Aperture:* f/11

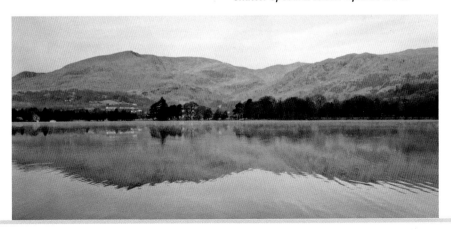

FUNCTIONS » SCENE MODES / USER-CONTROL MODES

THE EXPANDED GUIDE   43

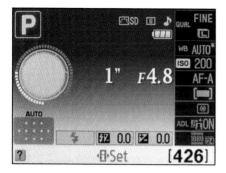

In **P** mode the camera sets a shutter speed and aperture combination that will give correctly exposed results in most situations. The same is true when using Full Auto and Scene Modes, but **P** allows you to adjust many other parameters to suit your own creative ideas.

1) To switch to Programmed auto mode, rotate the Mode dial to position **P**.

2) Frame the picture.

3) Half-depress the release button to activate focusing and exposure. The active focus point(s) will be displayed in the viewfinder image and the shutter speed and aperture settings will appear below the viewfinder image.

4) Fully depress the shutter release to take the picture.

Flexible program

Without leaving **P** mode you can change the shutter speed and aperture combination by rotating the Command Dial. Flexible program (sometimes called *program shift*) does not change the overall exposure level, so it won't make the image darker or lighter. Instead, it allows you to select a different shutter speed (if you want to freeze action, for example), or an alternative aperture for control over the depth of field.

While flexible program is in effect the **P** indication in the Information Display changes to **P***. A similar indication also appears in the viewfinder, and the shutter speed/aperture combination can be seen to change.

> **TIP**
>
> *As the D3100's Flexible program option allows you to adjust the paired aperture and shutter speed combination, Programmed auto gives you much the same control as the **A** or **S** modes.*

APERTURE PRIORITY »
Aperture Priority mode is ideal when you want to control the depth of field.
ISO: 200 *Focal Length:* 50mm
Shutter Speed: 1/1800 sec. *Aperture:* f/5.6

› Aperture Priority (A)

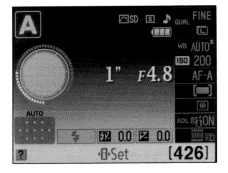

In Aperture Priority (**A**) mode, you control the aperture while the camera sets an appropriate shutter speed to give you a correctly exposed result in most situations. As the aperture is in the lens, not the camera, the range of apertures that is available is determined by the lens you have fitted. This means the choice of lens can be important because the aperture

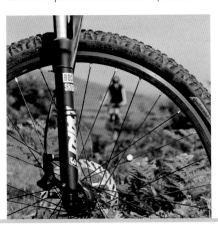

setting regulates the depth of field. Fine-tuning of the exposure is possible through the exposure lock and exposure compensation controls.

1) To switch to Aperture Priority, rotate the mode dial to **A**.

2) Frame the picture.

3) Half-depress the release button to activate focusing and exposure. The active focus point(s) will be displayed in the viewfinder, along with the shutter speed and aperture settings.

4) Rotate the Command Dial to adjust the aperture and the shutter speed will adjust automatically. The Information Display (in Graphic mode) also shows a graphic representation of the aperture.

5) Fully depress the shutter release to take the picture.

Exposure warning

If the aperture you have set requires a shutter speed that is beyond the camera's range, or is too slow for handheld shooting, exposure warnings will be displayed in both the viewfinder and the Information Display. When this happens, adjust the aperture until you achieve an acceptable shutter speed, fit a different lens with a wider maximum aperture, or adjust the ISO.

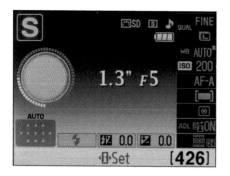

In Shutter Priority (**S**) mode, you control the shutter speed while the camera sets the aperture needed to give you a correctly exposed result. Control of the shutter speed is particularly useful when dealing with moving subjects and the D3100 allows shutter speeds between 30 seconds and 1/4000 sec. to be set. Fine-tuning of the exposure is possible through exposure lock and exposure compensation, with complete freedom to use flash, or not, as you wish.

SHUTTER PRIORITY

Shutter Priority auto allows direct control of the shutter speed for specific effects.

ISO: 160 *Focal Length:* 30mm
Shutter Speed: 1/500 sec. *Aperture:* f/13

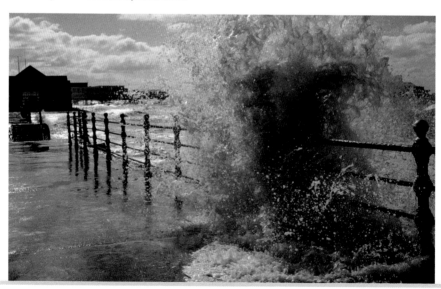

› Manual (**M**)

Scene Modes and shutter speed

Sports mode may aim to set a fast shutter speed, but it does not give the direct and exact control that **S** mode does. Nor does it allow quick shifts to a much slower shutter speed, which can be a great way to get a more impressionistic view of action.

1) To select Shutter Priority, rotate the mode dial to position **S**.

2) Frame the picture.

3) Half-depress the release button to activate focusing and exposure. The active focus point(s) will be displayed in the viewfinder image and the shutter speed and aperture settings will appear below the viewfinder image.

4) Rotate the Command Dial to alter the shutter speed. The aperture will change automatically.

5) Fully depress the shutter release to take the picture.

Exposure warning

If the shutter speed you've set requires an aperture that is unavailable with the lens in use, an exposure warning will be displayed. To resolve this, adjust the selected shutter speed until you achieve an acceptable aperture, fit a different lens with a different minimum/maximum aperture setting, or adjust the ISO sensitivity.

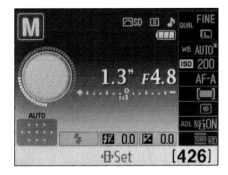

In Manual (**M**) mode, you control both the shutter speed and aperture for maximum creative flexibility. Manual mode is most comfortably employed when shooting without the pressure of time or in fairly constant lighting conditions. Many experienced photographers use it habitually to retain complete control.

Shutter speeds can be set at all values from 30 seconds to 1/4000 sec. and there's also the option to choose **B** (or "bulb"), which allows the shutter to remain open for as long as the shutter release is

> ### Tip
>
> *Manual mode is the only mode that allows the **B** (bulb) setting to be used, and therefore the only mode that allows exposure times longer than 30 seconds.*

depressed. As with Aperture Priority, the range of apertures that can be set is determined by the lens in use.

1) To use Manual mode, rotate the mode dial to position **M**.

2) Frame the picture.

3) Half-depress the release button to activate focusing and exposure. The shutter speed, aperture, and active focus point(s) will all be displayed in the viewfinder. Check the analog exposure display in the center of the viewfinder readouts and, if necessary, adjust the shutter speed, aperture, or both, to achieve the correct exposure.

4) Rotate the command dial to adjust the shutter speed.

5) Hold 🔳 and rotate the command dial to change the aperture setting.

6) Fully depress the shutter release to take the picture.

Using the analog exposure displays

In Manual mode, an analog exposure display appears in the center of the viewfinder readout and in the Information Display if it's active. This shows whether the photograph would be under- or overexposed at the current settings. The aim is to adjust the shutter speed and/or aperture until the indicator is aligned with the **0** mark in the center of the display: the exposure then matches the camera's recommendation. The quality of the D3100's metering is such that this will generally be correct, but if time allows it is always useful to review the image and check the histogram after taking the shot. If necessary, you can make further adjustments for creative effect, or adjust the settings if you feel the camera's recommended exposure does not achieve the desired result.

SWITCHING TO MANUAL   »
For this tricky subject I used Manual mode and checked the histogram display on playback.

ISO: 250
Focal Length: 150mm
Shutter Speed: 1/640 sec.
Aperture: f/20

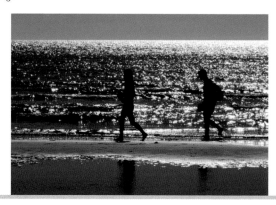

» METERING MODES

Nikon's metering system has long been admired and the D3100 provides three different metering modes that should cover any eventuality. You can switch between them using the Metering option in the Active Information Display, although this is only possible in the **P, A, S**, or **M** modes: in all other modes Matrix Metering is automatically selected.

› 3D Color Matrix Metering II ▣

Using a 420-segment color sensor, 3D Color Matrix Metering II analyzes data based on the brightness, color, and contrast of the scene. When used with Type G or Type D Nikkor lenses, the system also uses distance information based on where the camera focuses—hence it being called "3D." With other CPU lenses, distance information is not used and metering automatically reverts to standard (non-3D) Color Matrix Metering II. Matrix metering is recommended for the vast majority of shooting situations and will generally produce excellent results.

Warning!

If an older lens without a built-in CPU is attached, none of the camera's metering modes will operate.

› Center-weighted metering ▣

This traditional metering pattern will be familiar to most photographers with experience of 35mm SLR cameras. The camera measures light from the entire image area, but gives greater importance to a central circle. Center-weighted metering is useful in areas such as portraiture, where the key subject often occupies the central portion of the frame.

› Spot metering ▣

In this mode the camera meters solely from a small, circular area. With the D3100, this circle is centered on the currently active focus point, which means you have the freedom to take a meter reading from an off-center subject. However, this does not apply if Auto-area AF (**AF-A**) is in use, when the metering point is the center of the frame.

Effective use of spot metering requires more experience than the other metering modes, but in critical conditions its accuracy is unrivalled. It is important to understand that spot metering attempts to reproduce the metered area as a midtone and this must be allowed for (by using exposure compensation, for example) if the subject is significantly darker or lighter.

2 » EXPOSURE COMPENSATION

The range of metering options, and the incredible sophistication of matrix metering in particular, means that the D3100 will produce accurate exposures under most conditions, but no camera is infallible. It certainly can't read your mind or anticipate your creative ideas.

All metering systems are still, to some extent, based on the assumption that key subject areas have a mid tonal value and should therefore be recorded as a midtone. Most photographers will have seen the consequences that sometimes follow from this, such as snow scenes appearing unduly dark. When very light tones dominate the scene, the metering will tend to reproduce them as midtones, so they will come out darker than they should be. Conversely, when dark tones dominate, the converse is true and images can appear too light.

In the days of film, considerable experience was needed to accurately anticipate the need for exposure compensation, but with their instant feedback on exposure, digital cameras smooth the learning curve. It is still helpful—time permitting—to check the image, and specifically the histogram, after shooting, as this makes it much easier to see when exposure compensation is required. Then, with experience, you can anticipate when exposure compensation may be needed.

The basic principle for exposure compensation is very simple: to make the subject lighter, increase the exposure by applying positive (+) compensation, and to make the subject darker (to keep dark tones looking dark), decrease the exposure by applying negative (-) compensation.

Tips

*Exposure compensation is only available in **P**, **A**, and **S** modes. In **M** mode the user has total control over the shutter speed and aperture, while exposure control is fully automatic in the Full Auto and Scene Modes.*

The Nikon manual suggests that exposure compensation is most appropriate when using center-weighted or spot metering. Obviously their view is that Matrix Metering will achieve the correct exposure all on its own—and generally it will. However, there is no reason not to use exposure compensation if Matrix Metering does not give the exact result you are looking for.

› Resetting exposure compensation

Remember to reset the exposure compensation when you've finished shooting a particular scene; otherwise exposure compensation will continue to apply, probably inappropriately, to subsequent shots. Exposure compensation is canceled when you switch to Full Auto or Scene Modes, but the camera remembers the compensation setting and restores it when you revert to a User-control mode—it does not reset automatically, even when the camera is switched off. However, like many other settings, it will be restored to zero if you select **Reset shooting options** in the Shooting menu.

Using Exposure compensation

1) Press ⊞ to set the negative or positive compensation required (between −5EV and +5EV). Alternatively, the Active Information Display can be used.

2) Release ⊞. The chosen exposure compensation value is shown in the Information Display. In the viewfinder, the **0** at the center of the analog exposure display flashes while compensation is in effect.

3) Take the picture as normal. If time allows, check that the result is satisfactory, ideally by using the D3100's histogram.

4) To restore normal exposure settings, repeat step 1 until the displayed value returns to **0.0**.

> ### *Tip*
>
> *Exposure compensation can be set in steps of ⅓EV. The best way to get an idea of how much difference this makes—how big the steps are—is to take a few shots and see: start with a difference of ±1EV.*

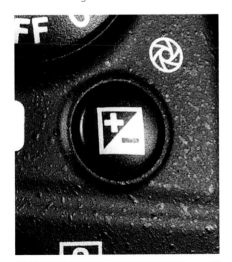

EXPOSURE COMPENSATION BUTTON ☆

2 › Exposure lock

Exposure lock is another way to fine-tune the camera's exposure setting and many users find this the quickest and most intuitive method. It's useful, for instance, in situations where very dark or light areas (especially light sources) within the frame can adversely influence the exposure. Exposure lock allows you to meter from a less extreme tonal area—by pointing the camera in a different direction or stepping closer to the subject, for example—then hold that exposure while re-framing the shot. Exposure lock can be used in all exposure modes.

Using Exposure lock
1) Aim the camera in a different direction, or zoom the lens to avoid the potentially problematic dark or light

> **Note:**
> Nikon does not recommend using exposure lock with Matrix Metering, and it probably does make most sense to use it with center-weighted or spot metering (where you want the camera to meter from a midtone). However, if there's a particular shot you want and Matrix Metering does not seem to give the desired result, there's no reason why you shouldn't try exposure lock. You can't damage anything, so the worst that can happen is that you still won't get exactly the right exposure.

area(s). If you're using center-weighted or spot metering, look for midtone areas that are receiving the same sort of light as the main subject.

2) Half-press the shutter-release button to take a meter reading and keep it held as you press the *AE-L/AF-L* button to lock the exposure value.

3) Continue to keep the *AE-L/AF-L* button half-pressed as you reframe the image and shoot in the normal way.

By default, the *AE-L/AF-L* button locks focus as well as exposure. This can be changed using the **Buttons** item in the Setup menu. There are several options, but the most relevant for using exposure lock is **AE Lock only**. You can also opt for **AE Lock (hold)**. In this case you can release the *AE-L/AF-L* button after step 2, and the exposure will remain locked until you press *AE-L/AF-L* again or the meter is turned off.

EXPOSURE BRACKETING IN ACTION »
Exposure bracketing covering a 3-stop range. From left to right, −1EV, 0, and +1EV.

ISO: 320 *Focal Length:* 21mm (with tripod)
Shutter Speed: various *Aperture:* f/13

› Exposure bracketing

A time-honored way of making sure that an image is correctly exposed is to take several frames at different exposures, and select the best one later—a practice known as *exposure bracketing*. Unlike other Nikon DSLRs, the D3100 does not have an automatic exposure bracketing facility, so this must be done manually.

In the **P**, **A**, and **S** exposure modes, the easiest way to employ manual exposure bracketing is to use exposure compensation. For example, take one shot at the metered exposure, another with the exposure compensation set at −1EV, and a third at +1EV. It is definitely quicker to use the ![±] button and Command Dial for this, rather than the Active Information Display and with a little practice it takes only a second or two to make three (or more) exposures.

In **M** mode you can bracket by directly changing either the aperture or shutter speed. For example, if the recommended exposure is 1/60 sec. at f/11, changing the shutter speed to 1/125 sec. is equivalent to −1EV, while changing it to 1/30 sec. is equivalent to +1EV.

Tip

Apart from acting as an insurance policy to ensure you have the "right" exposure for any given shot, experimenting with exposure bracketing is a great way to get a feel for what exposure really means. Use a tripod to make absolutely certain that your shots are all framed the same.

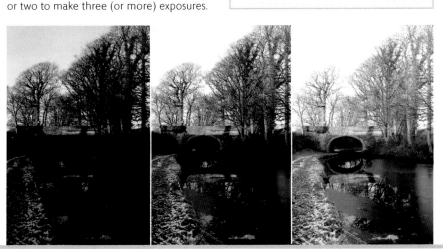

2 » FOCUSING

Focusing is not simply about making sure that the picture is "in focus." It's actually quite difficult, and often impossible, to ensure that everything in an image appears in sharp focus, so the first step is to make sure that the camera focuses on the desired subject or—especially with close-up photography—the right *part* of the subject. Controlling the depth of field will then help to determine how much of the rest of the scene will also appear sharp.

To secure focus on the desired subject, the D3100 has flexible and powerful focusing capabilities, offering manual focus, plus a range of autofocus modes.

To select the focus mode

1) In the Active Information Display, select the focus mode item. By default this reads (**AF-A**), which is about half way down the right side. Alternatively, use the **AF-area mode** option in the Shooting menu.

2) Press (**OK**) and then select from the available options; press (**OK**) again to confirm the selection and return to shooting mode.

If the camera is in a Full Auto or Scene Mode, the Active Information Display only shows two focus options. Manual focus can always be selected, but the only autofocus

option is **AF-A**. In **P**, **A**, **S**, or **M** mode, four options are available:

› Auto-servo AF (AF-A)

By default the camera is set to **AF-A** in all exposure modes. **AF-A** means that the camera automatically switches between two autofocus modes: **Single-servo AF (AF-S)** and **Continuous-servo AF (AF-C)**.

› Single-servo AF (AF-S)

AF-S can only be selected directly when the camera is in **P**, **S**, **A** or **M** mode. The camera focuses when the shutter release is pressed halfway. Focus remains locked on this point as long as the shutter release remains depressed. The shutter cannot release to take a picture unless focus has been acquired *(focus priority)*. This mode is recommended for accurate focusing on static subjects.

› Continuous-servo AF (AF-C)

In this mode, the camera continues to seek focus for as long as the shutter release is depressed. If the subject moves during this time then the camera will refocus accordingly to maintain sharpness. The camera is able to take a picture even if perfect focus has not been acquired.

The D3100 employs predictive focus tracking, meaning that if the subject moves while **AF-C** is active, the camera analyzes its movement and attempts to predict where it will be when the shutter is released. This mode is recommended for moving subjects, but can only be selected directly when the camera is in **P**, **A**, **S**, or **M** mode. In other modes, or if **AF-A** has been selected, the camera will only employ **AF-C** when it detects a moving subject.

› Manual focus (M)

The D3100's sophisticated AF capabilities might appear to make manual focus redundant, but many photographers still value the extra control and involvement that it offers. You may also have older lenses that don't support autofocus on the D3100. There are also certain subjects and circumstances that can confuse even the best AF systems—very low contrast or single-color subjects, for example.

The process hardly requires description: select Manual focus mode, then use the focusing ring on the lens to bring the subject into focus.

> ### Tip
>
> *Some lenses have an A/M switch for Auto and Manual focus: make sure this is set to **M** to use manual focus.*

The electronic rangefinder

When using a lens that does not focus automatically with the D3100, you can still take advantage of the camera's focusing technology thanks to the electronic rangefinder, which gives confirmation when a subject is in focus. Focusing this way may be more precise than just relying on the viewfinder image.

The electronic rangefinder is inactive by default, so to make it active, select **Rangefinder** in the Setup menu. Select **ON** and press (OK). Select an appropriate focus area, as if you were using autofocus, and then focus manually. When the subject in that area is in focus a green dot appears at the far left of the viewfinder data display.

› AF-area modes

The D3100 has 11 focus points, which are indicated by small black rectangles in the viewfinder. When you half-press the shutter release, the currently active focus point(s) are highlighted in red.

When using autofocus, the AF-area mode determines which of these focus points the camera will employ—in other words, the point that the camera will focus on. Auto-area is the default setting in most shooting modes, but can always be changed. However, the camera only "remembers" this change in **P**, **A**, **S**, or **M** modes. If you change AF-area mode in any of the Full Auto or Scene Modes it will remain in effect only as long as you remain in that exposure mode. For instance, if you switch from Portrait to Landscape and then back again, you will find that the camera has reverted to Auto-area AF.

As many photographers prefer to make their own selection (determining where the subject is seems a pretty basic decision) the AF-area mode options can be selected in the Shooting menu or via the Active Information Display.

› Auto-area AF **AF-A**

Set to Auto-area AF, the D3100 selects the focus point automatically. In effect, the camera is deciding what the intended subject is and when Type G or Type D lenses are used, Face Recognition allows the D3100 to distinguish human subject(s) from their background.

› Single-point AF [⊏⊐]

In this mode, you select the focus area, using the multi-selector to move through the eleven focus points. The chosen focus

point is outlined in the viewfinder. This mode is best suited to subjects that are relatively static.

› Dynamic-area AF [⋅⊏⊐⋅]

Dynamic-area AF is a little more complicated than the others, as its operation changes depending on whether **AF-S** or **AF-C** is selected. In **AF-S** mode its operation is essentially the same as Single-point AF, but it comes into its own when using **AF-C** mode.

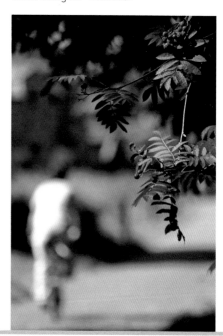

PICKING THE POINT OF FOCUS »
The shot was deliberately focused on the rowan berries, but it was important that the cyclist should still be recognizable as such.

ISO: 160 *Focal Length:* 200mm (tripod)
Shutter Speed: 1/60 sec. *Aperture:* f/5.6

The initial focus point is still selected by the user, but if the subject moves, the camera will activate additional points to maintain focus. This mode is naturally suited to moving subjects, particularly if they remain in line with the initial focus point. For erratically moving subjects, 3D-tracking is recommended.

› 3D-tracking (11 points)

When using **AF-C**, you still select the initial focus point for 3D-tracking, but if the subject moves, the focusing system uses a wide range of information—including subject colors—to maintain focus. You must keep the shutter-release semi-depressed for this to apply and if the subject and background are similar in color, 3D-tracking may prove unreliable. 3D-tracking is not available in **AF-S** mode.

DYNAMIC-AREA AF ☆
Dynamic-area AF tracks moving subjects.

ISO: 320 *Focal Length:* 150mm
Shutter Speed: 1/250 sec. *Aperture:* f/5.6

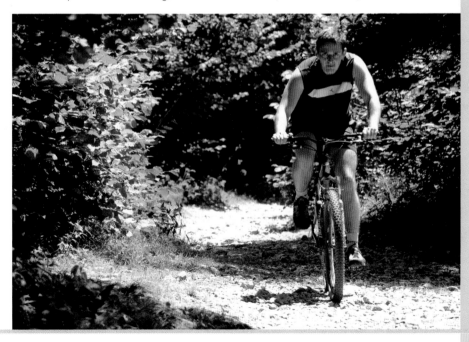

› Focus points

Early autofocus cameras were rightly criticized for limiting the point of focus to the center of the frame or to a small number of points. With eleven focus points covering most of the frame, the D3100 is far more flexible, making it possible to quickly and precisely focus on any subject with accuracy.

1) Make sure the camera is set to an AF-area mode other than **Auto-area**.

2) Half-depress the shutter-release button to activate the autofocus system.

3) Using the multi-selector, select the desired focus point, which will be highlighted in red.

4) Press the shutter-release button halfway to focus at the desired point, then depress it fully to take the shot.

SELECTING A FOCUS POINT

I selected the focus point manually to be sure that focus was on the flowers in the foreground.

ISO: 125 ***Focal Length:*** 26mm
Shutter Speed: 1/160 sec. ***Aperture:*** f/11

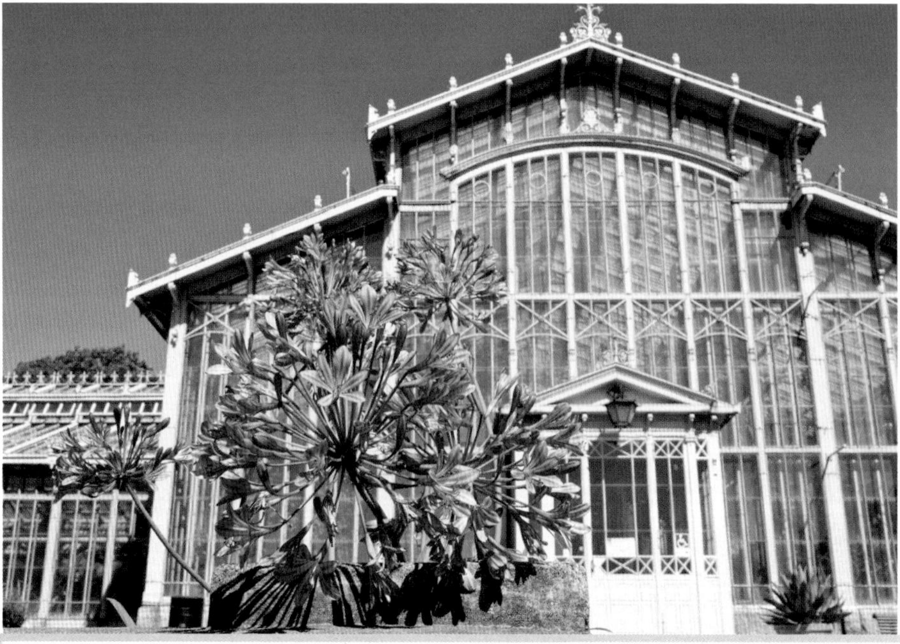

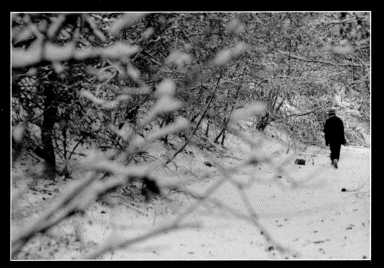

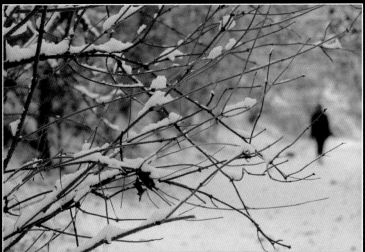

SHIFTING FOCUS ⌃
Shifting the focus point gives very different results from the same view.

ISO: 200 *Focal Length:* 85mm
Shutter Speed: 1/200 sec. *Aperture:* f/4

Although the D3100's focus points cover a wide area, they do not extend to the edges of the frame, and sometimes you may need to focus on a subject that does not naturally coincide with any of the focus points. To do this, the simplest procedure is as follows:

1) Adjust the framing so that the subject falls within the available focus area.

2) Select an appropriate focus point and focus on the subject by half-depressing the shutter-release button.

3) Lock focus. In Single-servo AF mode, this can be done either by keeping half-pressure on the shutter-release button, or by pressing and holding the **AE-L/AF-L** button. An **AE-L** icon appears in the viewfinder.

In Continuous-Servo AF, only **AE-L/AF-L** can be used to lock focus.

4) Reframe the image as desired and press the shutter-release button fully to take the picture. If half-pressure is maintained on the shutter-release button (in Single-Servo AF), or the **AE-L/AF-L** button is kept under pressure (in either AF mode), focus will remain locked for subsequent shots.

> **Note:**
> By default, the **AE-L/AF-L** button locks the exposure as well as the focus, but this can be changed using the **Buttons** item in the Setup menu.

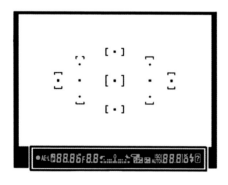

THE D3100 VIEWFINDER «
The viewfinder displays the available focus areas as well as an in-focus indicator at the left of the menu bar.

› AF–Assist illuminator

An AF-assist illuminator—a long name for a small lamp—is available to help the D3100 focus in dim light. It requires the camera to be in **AF-S** mode and will then illuminate automatically when required, except in Landscape and Sports modes, where it is disabled. The AF-assist illuminator can be turned **OFF** for all modes using the **AF-assist** option in the Shooting menu and it is also deactivated during Live View and Movie shooting.

For effective operation, the lens focal length should be in the range 18–200mm and the subject distance should be 1ft 8in–9ft 10in (0.5–3m).

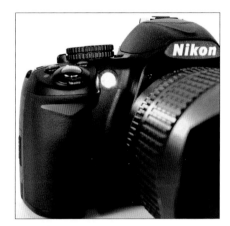

AF-ASSIST ILLUMINATOR ☆

Tips

Some lens hoods can block the light from the AF-assist illuminator; if the camera has difficulty focusing in low light, try removing the lens hood to avoid this.

Some lenses are partly or wholly incompatible with the AF-assist illuminator—see the D3100's manual for details.

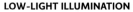

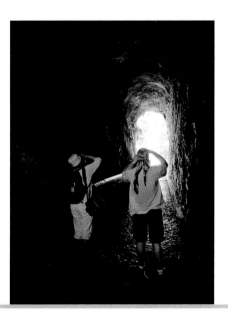

LOW-LIGHT ILLUMINATION »
The AF-assist illuminator allows the D3100 to focus in dim light.

ISO: 2500 ***Focal Length:*** 12mm
Shutter Speed: 1/40 sec. ***Aperture:*** f/14

2 » IMAGE QUALITY

Image-quality settings are not some miraculous way of ensuring great pictures; that is still ultimately down to the eye of the photographer. Instead, "image quality" refers to the file format, which is the way in which image data is recorded.

The D3100 offers a choice of two file types: NEF (RAW) and JPEG. These are substantially different and the choice of which one you use has major implications both for how you shoot and what you do with your images afterward.

The essential difference is that JPEG images are extensively processed in the camera to produce photographs that should be usable immediately (for direct printing from the memory card, for example), and need little or no further processing on computer.

NEF files, on the other hand, record the raw data from the camera's sensor "as is,"

without processing in the camera. This leaves much greater scope for processing on the computer to achieve the desired pictorial result, although it requires sophisticated software such as *Nikon Capture NX2* or *Adobe Photoshop* to achieve the best results. Because they preserve the raw data, the generic term for this kind of file is RAW—NEF is a specific file format used by Nikon for its own RAW files (Canon uses CR2, for example).

As a further refinement, the D3100 allows two versions of the same image to be recorded simultaneously, one RAW and one JPEG. The JPEG can be used as a quick reference file for immediate needs, while the RAW version can be processed later for the ultimate result.

There are three JPEG quality options, which determine the level of compression applied when the file is saved. A higher level of compression produces smaller file sizes, so more pictures will fit on a memory card, but it can degrade the image quality. **Fine** produces the largest file sizes at the highest quality; **Basic** produces the smallest files at a lower quality; **Normal** is between the two.

Setting image quality

1) In the Active Information Display, select **QUAL** at top right of the screen.

> ### *Tip*
>
> *Image quality is set to **Normal** by default. Unless you need to shoot huge numbers of images on a single memory card, or you know for certain that none of your images will ever be made into large prints, change this setting to **Fine** and keep all your options open.*

2) Press (OK) to bring up the list of options. Use the multi-selector to highlight the required setting and press (OK) to make it effective.

› Image size

With JPEG files, the D3100 offers three image-size options: **Large** is the maximum available size from the D3100's sensor, producing images measuring 4608 x 3072 pixels, **Medium** images measure 3456 x 2304 pixels (roughly equivalent to an 8-megapixel camera), and **Small** produces images measuring 2304 x 1536 pixels (roughly equivalent to a 3.5-megapixel camera). **Small** size images comfortably exceed the maximum resolution of an HD

TV or most computer monitors and can yield good prints up to around 10 x 7 inches (printed at 200 dpi), but for most applications, **Large** is the best option.

Setting image size

Image size only applies to JPEG images so you will not be able to select this option if the image quality is set to RAW or RAW+FINE.

1) In the Active Information Display, select **Image size** at the top right of the screen or select **Image size** from the Shooting menu.

2) Press (OK) to bring up the list of options. Use the multi-selector to highlight the required setting and then press (OK) to select it.

Image quality options	
RAW	12-bit NEF (RAW) files are recorded for the ultimate quality and creative flexibility.
FINE	8-bit JPEG files are recorded with a compression ratio of approx 1:4. Suitable for prints of Tabloid/A3 size or even larger.
NORM	8-bit JPEG files are recorded with a compression ratio of approx 1:8. Suitable for Letter/A4-sized prints.
BASIC	8-bit JPEG files are recorded with a compression ratio of approx 1:16. Suitable for transmission by email or website use, but not recommended for printing.
RAW + F	Two copies of the same image are recorded simultaneously: one NEF (RAW) and one JPEG Fine.

2 » WHITE BALANCE

All light sources, both natural and artificial, vary enormously in color. The human eye and brain are very good (though not perfect) at compensating for this and seeing people and objects in their "true" colors, so that we nearly always see grass as green, and so on. In the days of film—especially slide film—achieving natural-looking colors often required the careful use of filters, but digital cameras have a far greater capacity to compensate for the varying colors of light. Used correctly, this means that the D3100 can produce natural-looking colors under almost any conditions you are likely to encounter.

The D3100 has a sophisticated system for determining the White Balance (**WB**)

automatically, which produces very good results most of the time. For finer control, or for creative effect, the D3100 also offers a range of user-controlled settings, but these are only accessible when using the **P**, **A**, **S**, or **M** modes.

> **Note:**
> *When shooting RAW images, the in-camera WB setting is not crucial, as white balance can also be adjusted in post-processing using suitable software. However, it is still helpful to get it right in camera as it affects how images look on playback and review.*

1   2   3

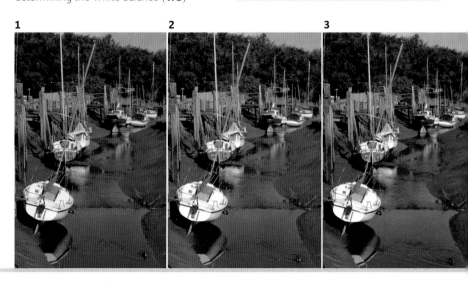

Tip

Sometimes you may not want to "correct" the colors in an image too much. A classic example is shooting a landscape in the warm light of early morning or late evening, where the reddened hue of the sunlight is part of the appeal. Auto White Balance may sometimes neutralize this effect, so try setting the WB to **Direct sunlight** *instead.*

WHITE BALANCE ⌄
1) Incandescent; **2**) Cool-white fluorescent;
3) Direct sunlight); **4**) Flash; **5**) Cloudy; **6**) Shade

› Setting white balance

There are two ways to set White Balance:

Using the Active Information Display
1) In the Active Information Display, select **WB** near the top right and press (**OK**) to reveal a list of options.

2) Use the multi-selector to highlight the required setting, then press (**OK**).

Using the Shooting menu
This is a slower method but makes extra options available.

1) Press **MENU**, select the **Shooting menu**, and navigate to **White Balance**.

2) Press (**OK**) to reveal a list of options.

5   6

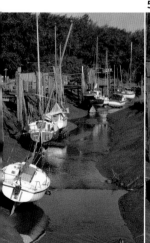
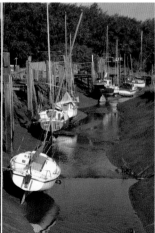
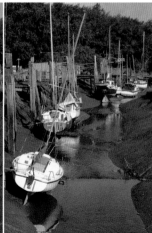

2

3) Use the multi-selector to highlight the required setting and press (OK).

4) In most cases, a graphical display appears that allows you to fine-tune the setting using the multi-selector, or you can press (OK) to accept the standard value. However, when you select **Fluorescent**, a sub-menu appears, from which you can select an appropriate type of fluorescent lamp.

> **Note:**
> *If you use the Active Information Display to select **Fluorescent**, the precise value will be whatever was last selected in the sub-menu under the Shooting menu. The default is 4: Cool-white fluorescent.*

Warning!

If your images consistently appear to have a color-shift when you view them on your computer screen, don't try and compensate by adjusting the camera's White Balance—the problem is far more likely to be with the monitor's settings.

> **Note:**
> *Energy-saving bulbs, which have extensively replaced traditional incandescent (tungsten) bulbs in domestic use, are compact fluorescent units. Their color temperature varies but many are rated around 2700K, which is equivalent to Fluorescent setting 1: Sodium-vapor lamps. With any unfamiliar light source it is always a good idea to take test shots if possible, or allow for adjustment later by shooting RAW files.*

› Fine-tuning Auto White Balance

If you access it through the Shooting menu, fine-tuning is possible with the Auto White Balance setting. This means the camera will adjust the White Balance according to different lighting conditions, but the results will be shifted in the direction you chose—for example, you may like your images to turn out consistently a little warmer than the camera makes them by default. This is only possible in **P**, **A**, **S**, or **M** exposure modes and the **AUTO** indication in menu or display screen changes to **AUTO*** to remind you that a change has been made.

ICON	MENU OPTION	COLOR TEMP.	DESCRIPTION
AUTO	AUTO	3500–8000K	Camera sets WB automatically, based on information from imaging and metering sensors. Most accurate with Type G and Type D lenses.
☀	Incandescent	3000K	Use in incandescent (tungsten) lighting, such as traditional household bulbs.

Fluorescent: (Sub-menu offers seven options):

ICON	MENU OPTION	COLOR TEMP.	DESCRIPTION
	1) Sodium-vapor lamps	2700K	Use in sodium-vapor lighting, often used in sports venues.
	2) Warm-white fluorescent	3000K	Use in warm-white fluorescent lighting.
	3) Warm fluorescent	3700K	Use in white fluorescent lighting.
☼	4) Cool-white fluorescent	4200K	Use in cool-white fluorescent lighting.
	5) Day-white fluorescent	5000K	Use in daylight white fluorescent lighting.
	6) Daylight fluorescent	6500K	Use in daylight fluorescent lighting.
	7) Mercury-vapor lamps	7200K	Use in high-color-temperature lighting, such as mercury-vapor lamps.
☀	Direct sunlight	5200K	Use for subjects in direct sunlight.
⚡	Flash	5400K	Use with built-in flash or separate flashgun. Value may require fine-tuning with large-scale studio flash.
☁	Cloudy	6000K	Use in daylight, under cloudy or overcast conditions.
🏠	Shade	8000K	Use on sunny days for subjects in shade.
PRE	Preset manual	n/a	Derive white balance direct from subject or light-source, or from an existing photograph.

2 » ISO SENSITIVITY SETTINGS

The ISO setting governs the camera's sensitivity to light. At higher ISO settings, less light is needed to capture an acceptable image, which will allow you to keep on shooting in low light, enable you to use a smaller aperture for increased depth of field, or select a fast shutter speed to freeze rapid movement. Conversely, lower ISO settings are useful in brighter conditions and/or when you want to use wide apertures or slow shutter speeds.

The D3100 offers settings from ISO 100 to ISO 3200, and while there is a tendency for image noise to increase at the higher settings, the D3100 controls it well. There are also additional settings of **Hi 1** (which is equivalent to ISO 6400) and **Hi 2** (equivalent to ISO 1280), although these are only tentatively recommended as image noise becomes far more noticeable.

Auto ISO sensitivity

By default, the D3100 sets the ISO automatically, but it is always possible to change to a manual setting in any exposure mode. In most instances, this new setting will apply even if you switch exposure modes, although if you switch to **P**, **A**, **S**, or **M** mode and then back to any of the Full Auto or Scene Modes, the camera reverts to Auto-ISO. The D3100 only permanently "remembers" manual ISO settings in the **P**, **A**, **S**, and **M** modes.

The **ISO sensitivity settings** option in the Shooting menu has a sub-menu called **Auto ISO sensitivity control**: if this is set to **ON**, the D3100 will automatically depart from a manually selected ISO if it determines that this is required for the correct exposure. Extra options within this menu allow you to limit the maximum ISO and minimum shutter speed that the camera can use when applying Auto ISO sensitivity control.

Setting the ISO

The usual way to set the **ISO** is through the Active Information Display:

1) In the Active Information Display, select ISO on the right and press (OK) to reveal a list of options.

2) Use the multi-selector to highlight the required ISO setting, and then press (OK) to accept it.

Alternatively, you can use the **ISO sensitivity settings** option in the Shooting menu.

A third method is available, which involves assigning the **Fn** button to **ISO sensitivity** through the **Buttons** option in the Setup menu. If this is done, pressing **Fn** brings up the ISO settings in the Active Information Display, allowing them to be changed quickly with the Command Dial.

For those who change ISO settings regularly, this is an option that is well worth considering.

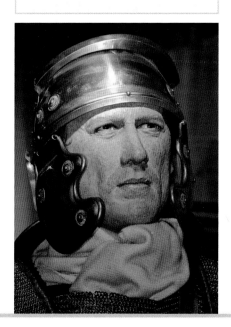

» COLOR SPACE

The color space defines the range (or *gamut*) of colors that can be recorded. Like most DSLRs, the Nikon D3100 offers a choice between sRGB and Adobe RGB color spaces, with the chosen color space applying to all shots taken in all exposure modes. sRGB (the default setting) has a narrower gamut than Adobe RGB, but images often appear brighter and punchier. It is the standard color space used on the Internet and by most photo printers so is a safe choice for images that are likely to be used or printed straight off, with little or no post-processing.

Adobe RGB has a wider gamut and is commonly used in professional printing and reproduction. It is a better choice for images that are destined for professional applications or where significant post-processing is anticipated.

To select the color space, choose **Color space** from the Shooting menu and pick either **sRGB** or **Adobe RGB**.

LOW-LIGHT, HIGH ISO «
This effigy was too tall to get the angle I wanted using a tripod, so to shoot handheld in the low light of the museum I had to set a high ISO.

ISO: 3200 *Focal Length:* 200mm
Shutter Speed: 1/160 sec. *Aperture:* f/10

2 » QUICK RESET

The D3100 offers a quick way to reset a large number of camera settings (listed below) to their default values. The top item in the Shooting menu is **Reset shooting options** and, similarly, the top item in the Setup menu is **Reset setup options**. In each case, select **Yes** and then press (OK) to reset a variety of options back to their default values. The range of settings covered by these reset options are listed *below*.

<table>
<tr><td colspan="3" align="center">RESET SHOOTING OPTIONS</td></tr>
<tr><td>ITEM</td><td colspan="2">DEFAULT SETTINGS</td></tr>
<tr><td>Set Picture Control</td><td colspan="2">Standard settings only</td></tr>
<tr><td>Image quality</td><td colspan="2">JPEG Normal</td></tr>
<tr><td>Image size</td><td colspan="2">Large (4608 x 3072 pixels)</td></tr>
<tr><td>White balance</td><td colspan="2">Auto (fine-tuning off)</td></tr>
<tr><td rowspan="3">ISO sensitivity</td><td>Auto and scene modes</td><td>Auto</td></tr>
<tr><td>User-control modes</td><td>100</td></tr>
<tr><td>Auto ISO sensitivity</td><td>100</td></tr>
<tr><td>Active D-Lighting</td><td colspan="2">On</td></tr>
<tr><td>Auto distortion control</td><td colspan="2">Off</td></tr>
<tr><td>Color space</td><td colspan="2">sRGB</td></tr>
<tr><td>Noise reduction</td><td colspan="2">On</td></tr>
<tr><td rowspan="3">AF-Area mode
(Viewfinder)</td><td>🌷</td><td>Single point AF</td></tr>
<tr><td>🏃</td><td>Dynamic Area AF</td></tr>
<tr><td>AUTO 📷 , 🚫 , 🏔 , ⛰ , ★ , 🌸, P, A, S, M</td><td>Auto-area AF</td></tr>
<tr><td rowspan="4">AF-Area mode
(Live View/Movie)</td><td>AUTO 📷 , 🚫 , 🏔 , ⛰ , ★ , 🌸</td><td>Face-priority AF</td></tr>
<tr><td>🏃 , P, A, S, M</td><td>Wide-area AF</td></tr>
<tr><td>🌷</td><td>Normal-area AF</td></tr>
</table>

AF-assist	On	
Metering	Matrix	
Movie Settings	Quality	1920 x 1080 pixels/24fps
	Sound	On
Built-in flash	TTL	
Focus point	Center	
Flexible program	Off	
AE-L/AF-L button hold	Off	
Focus mode	Viewfinder	AF-A
	Live View/movie	AF-S
Flash mode	AUTO 📷 , 🎭 , 🌷 , 🏔	Auto
	📷★	Auto slow sync
	P, A, S, M	Front-curtain sync
Exposure compensation	Off	
Flash compensation	Off	

RESET SHOOTING OPTIONS

ITEM	DEFAULT SETTINGS	
LCD brightness	0	
Info display format	Graphic (background color green)	
Self-timer delay	10 seconds	
Beep	On	
Rangefinder	Off	
Buttons	**Fn**	ISO sensitivity
	AE-L/AF-L	AE/AF lock
	AE lock	Off
Date imprint	Off	
Eye-Fi upload	Enable	

2 » LIVE VIEW

Live View mode allows you to frame your pictures using the LCD screen rather than the viewfinder, just as many compact digital camera users habitually do. However, on a DSLR, Live View is an adjunct to the viewfinder, not a substitute for it. The SLR is essentially designed around the viewfinder, which is far superior for the majority of picture taking. However, Live View can prove invaluable under certain conditions, most notably when it's awkward to use the viewfinder, such as when you are working very close to the ground. It can also prove beneficial when ultra-precise focusing is required.

Live View is also the jumping-off point for shooting movies with the D3100, which has its own chapter later in this book. However, familiarity with Live View is a big advantage when it comes to preparing for movie shooting.

Using Live View

To activate Live View, flick and release the **LV** switch on the rear of the camera. The

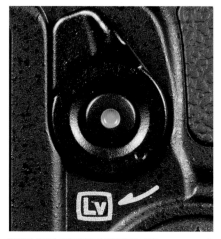

LIVE VIEW ACTIVATION SWITCH　　　　　⌃

viewfinder mirror flips up, the viewfinder blacks out, and the rear monitor screen displays a continuous live preview of the scene. A range of shooting information is displayed at the top and bottom of the screen, partly overlaying the image. Pressing **info** changes this Information Display, cycling through a series of screens as outlined in the table below.

LIVE VIEW INFO	DETAILS
Show indicators (default)	Information bars superimposed at the top and bottom of the screen.
Hide indicators	Top information bar disappears, but key shooting information is still shown at the bottom.
Framing grid	Grid lines appear, which are useful for critical framing.

› Focusing in Live View

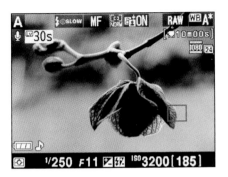

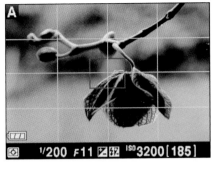

To take a picture, you press the shutter-release button fully (as when shooting normally), but it is worth noting that if you are in Continuous shooting mode the monitor remains blank between shots, making it hard to follow moving subjects.

If an Auto or Scene Mode is selected, exposure control is fully automatic, except that the exposure level can be locked using the **AE-L/AF-L** button. In **P**, **A**, **S**, or **M** modes, exposure levels can be adjusted by ±5EV using the ⎇ button, and the Live View display changes to reflect this. The shutter speed and aperture settings can also be changed in the usual way, although the Live View display does not change, as the overall exposure should remain constant: the numerical indicators at the bottom of the display will be adjusted, though. To exit Live View flick the **LV** switch again.

Because the mirror is locked up, the usual focusing sensor is unavailable in Live View, so the camera takes its focus information directly from the main imaging sensor. This is significantly slower than normal AF operation, and another reason why Live View is not suitable for fast-moving subjects. It is, however, very accurate.

Live View has its own set of autofocus options, with two AF modes and four AF-area modes, as described on the following pages.

Tip

You can zoom into the Live View, although on the D3100 this appears to magnify the relevant section of the full-screen image without gaining resolution. This reduces, but does not completely eliminate, the value of the zoom for a critical focus check.

› Live View AF mode

The Live View AF options are Single-servo AF (**AF-S**) and Full-time servo AF (**AF-F**). AF-S corresponds to AF-S in normal shooting: the camera focuses when the shutter release is pressed halfway, and focus remains locked as long as the shutter release remains depressed.

AF-F corresponds roughly to AF-C in normal shooting. However, the camera continues to seek focus as long as Live View remains active. When the shutter-release button is pressed halfway the focus will lock, and remains locked until the button is released, or a shot is taken.

Select your preferred Live View AF mode as follows:

1) Activate Live View with the **LV** switch.

2) Press ◀**🛈**▶ to engage the Active Information Display and select between **AF-S** and **AF-F** (midway down the right side of the display).

3) Press ◀**🛈**▶ again to return to Live View. Alternatively, the Live View AF mode can be selected in the Shooting menu.

NORMAL AREA AF »
Normal area AF is the best choice for precise and accurate focusing in Live View mode.

ISO: 400 *Focal Length:* 70mm
Shutter Speed: 1/60 sec. *Aperture:* f/5.6

› Live View AF-area mode

AF-area modes determine how the focus point is selected. Live View AF-area modes do not correspond to the ones used in normal shooting, so see the table *opposite* for details of the Live View AF-area modes. Again, selection is through the Active Information Display and you can select the Live View AF-area mode as follows:

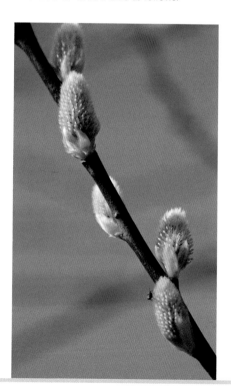

AF MODE	DESCRIPTION
😊 Face priority	Uses face-detection technology to identify portrait subjects. Double yellow border appears outlining such subjects. If multiple subjects are detected the camera focuses on the closest. Default in 🤸 , 🏔 , 🧑‍🎨, and 🎭 .
⟦⟧ WIDE Wide-area	Camera analyzes focus information from an area approximately the width and height of the frame; area is shown by a red rectangle. Default in 🌷 .
⟦⟧ NORM Normal area	Camera analyzes focus information from a much smaller area, shown by a red rectangle. Useful for precise focusing on small subjects. Default in 🏃 .
⊕ Subject tracking	Camera follows the selected subject as it moves within the frame

1) Activate Live View with the **LV** switch.

2) Press ◄🔘► to engage the Active Information Display and select the AF-area mode (midway down the right side of the display).

3) Press ◄🔘► again to return to Live View. Alternatively, Live View AF mode can be selected in the Shooting menu.

> ## Using Live View AF

⟦⟧ WIDE Wide-area AF/⟦⟧ NORM Normal area AF

In both of these AF-area modes, the focus point (outlined in red) can be moved anywhere on the screen, using the multi-selector. Pressing ⊕ zooms the screen view—press repeatedly to zoom closer. Helpfully, the zoom centers on the focus point. Once the focus point is set, autofocus is activated by half-pressing the shutter-release button, with the red rectangle turning green when focus is achieved.

2

[☺] Face-priority AF

When this mode is active, the camera automatically detects up to five faces and selects the closest. The selected face is outlined with a double yellow border. You can override this and focus on a different person by using the multi-selector to shift the focus point. To focus on the selected face, half-press the shutter-release button.

[⊕] Subject tracking

When Subject tracking is selected, a white rectangle appears at the center of the screen. Align this with the desired subject using the multi-selector and press **OK**. The camera "memorizes" the subject and the focus target turns yellow. It will now track the subject as it moves, and can even reacquire the subject if it temporarily leaves the frame.

To focus, press the shutter- halfway; the target rectangle blinks green as the camera focuses and then becomes solid green. If the camera fails to focus the rectangle will blink red instead. Pictures can still be taken, but focus may not be correct. To end focus tracking press **OK** again.

Manual focus

Manual focus is engaged as in normal shooting. However, the Live View display continues to reflect the previously selected Live View AF mode. It's helpful to have Wide-area AF or Normal-area AF selected, as the display still shows a rectangle of the appropriate size. If you zoom in for more precise focusing, the zoom centers on the area defined by the rectangle.

Screen brightness

Press and hold **?** and use ▲ and ▼ to alter screen brightness in Live View.

> *Note:*
> *This only affects screen brightness; it has no effect on the exposure level of images. To verify exposure, use the playback review.*

Warning!

Subject tracking in Live View mode isn't fast enough for rapidly moving subjects. Using the viewfinder is much more effective for these types of subject.

» GUIDE MODE

The D3000 was the first DSLR to feature the Guide Mode, and the D3100 extends its range. Guide Mode is selected from the Mode Dial in the same way as all of the other exposure options, but it is not in itself an exposure mode. Instead, Guide Mode is intended, as the name suggests, to guide inexperienced users through some of the available options; not only for shooting, but also for playback and camera setup. The word "some" is significant, as while the Guide Mode caters for many common scenarios, it falls short of covering all of the subjects that the D3100 can tackle.

› Guide Menu

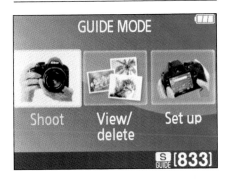

To enter Guide Mode, rotate the Mode Dial to **GUIDE** and the Guide Menu screen will appear. To return to this screen if the monitor turns off, or from the Information Display, press **MENU**. This only works while the Mode Dial is in the **GUIDE** position. The Guide Menu offers three initial choices: **Shoot, View/Delete**, and **Setup**. Initially, **Shoot** is highlighted, but you can use ◀ and ▶ to select an alternative option before pressing ⑥ⓚ to enter.

› Guide Menu: Shoot

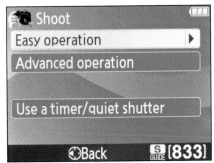

The Shoot screen offers three options: **Easy operation, Advanced operation**, and **Use a timer/quiet shutter**. Move between them with ▲ and ▼ ; use ▶ or ⑥ⓚ to enter.

2

Easy operation

Enter Easy operation and the camera offers a new set of options, as shown in the table below. Each of these leads to one of the Full Auto or Scene Modes, although the Guide Menu uses different terminology for some of them. Once you're familiar with the Scene Modes themselves, it should be obvious that selecting them directly through the Mode Dial is a far quicker method than using the Guide Menu—it takes a minimum of five button-presses, and usually some operation of the multi-selector to make a selection from the Guide Menu!

	GUIDE MENU—EASY OPERATION		
GUIDE MENU HEADING	EXPOSURE MODE	NOTES	FLASH SELECTION
Auto	AUTO Auto		Available
No flash	Auto (flash off)		Unavailable
Distant subjects	Sports	Uses Sports mode to maintain a fast shutter-speed, preventing camera-shake with long lenses.	Unavailable
Close-ups	Close up		Available
Sleeping faces	Child	Unlike the Child mode set on the Mode Dial, the flash is **Off** by default, but can be activated from the **More settings** menu.	Available
Moving subjects	Sports		Unavailable
Landscapes	Landscape		Unavailable
Portraits	Portrait		Available
Night portrait	Night portrait		Available

Advanced operation

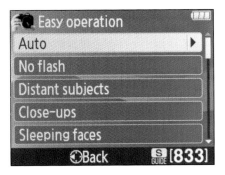

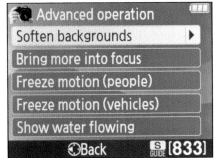

Once you've selected a mode through the Guide Menu, there's one final screen. Select **Start shooting** if you're ready, or choose **More settings** and press (OK) to access options that include **Release mode, AF-area mode**, and, in most cases, the **Flash mode**.

As you scroll through the available options the Guide Menu provides a brief explanation and an image of an appropriate subject. Having made any changes that you want to, scroll down to **Start shooting** and press (OK) to choose whether you want to **Use the viewfinder, Use live view**, or **Shoot movies**.

If you select **Advanced operation** you are offered five choices. **Soften backgrounds** and **Bring more into focus** both take you into Aperture Priority (**A**) mode, while **Freeze motion (people), Freeze motion (vehicles)**, and **Show water flowing** activate Shutter Priority (**S**) mode. In each case there's an explanatory screen.

In **Soften backgrounds**, the camera advises fitting a lens of at least 80mm and sets a fairly wide aperture to minimize the depth of field, while **Bring more into focus** advises fitting a lens of 24mm or wider, and sets a fairly small aperture to maximize the depth of field. While the Guide screen is showing, the aperture can be adjusted using ▲ and ▼. Once you start shooting, further changes to the aperture can be made using the Command Dial in the usual way.

2

Aperture numbers are really fractions, so f/16 is a small aperture while f/4 is large. They should always be written as fractions—so f/8 not f8—but the D3100's Guide Mode screens and Information Display fail to do so. However, these screens, and the Information Display (in Graphic mode), do contain a graphic that corresponds to the lens aperture, which can be seen to get bigger as the numbers get smaller.

Freeze motion (people) and **Freeze motion (vehicles)** are basically the same, except that the camera sets an initial shutter speed of 1/200 sec. for people and 1/1000 sec. for vehicles. This is all very well, but 1/200 sec. isn't going to give you a sharp image of Usain Bolt in full cry, while 1/1000 sec. could be more than fast enough for some slower-moving vehicles. The implicit assumption that vehicles need a faster shutter speed than people is naive, but you have to start somewhere!

Show water flowing suggests a shutter speed of 1 second or slower to produce a smooth, silky effect in flowing water, so a tripod is essential.

Further options

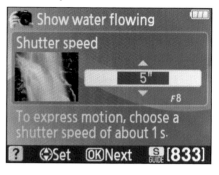

Having accepted or changed the suggested aperture/shutter speed, pressing **OK** takes you to a screen where you can choose **Start shooting** or **More settings**. Select the latter and there are further options: **Set Picture Control**, **Exposure compensation**, and **Flash compensation**. Having worked through (or passed over) these, choose **Start shooting** or press **Next** to bring up three more sets of options: **Flash mode**, **Release mode**, and **AF-area mode**: these are the same as in Easy operation.

Use a timer/quiet shutter

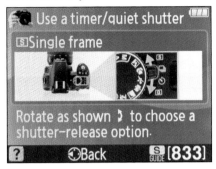

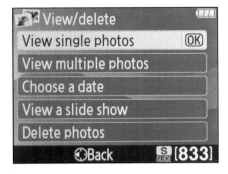

The name of this guide menu item is potentially a little misleading: it actually covers the full range of Release-mode options. In fact, all it does is show you where the Release-mode selector is, and give the full name of each release mode to go with the icon on the selector.

This section of the Guide Menu offers an alternative way to access some of the D3100's playback functions. These are all described on the following pages under **Image playback** and **Playback menu** so there's no need to repeat the information here. The Guide Menu headings are:

View single photo *(see page 86)*

View multiple photos *(see page 87)*

Choose a date *(see page 87)*

View a slide show *(see page 96)*

Delete photos *(see page 85)*

2 › Guide Menu: Set up

This section of the Guide Menu gives access to a range of settings that would otherwise be accessed through the Playback menu, Shooting menu and Set up menu; a couple are also accessible through the Active Information Display.

THE GUIDE MENU: SET UP OPTIONS

GUIDE MENU	NORMAL MENU LOCATION	ACCESSIBLE THROUGH ACTIVE INFORMATION DISPLAY?
Image quality	Shooting menu	Yes
Image size	Shooting menu	Yes
Playback folder	Playback menu	No
Print set (DPOF)	Playback menu	No
Format memory card	Setup menu	No
LCD brightness	Setup menu	No
Info background color	Setup menu	No
Auto info display	Setup menu	No
Video mode	Setup menu	No
Time zone and date	Setup menu	No
Language	Setup menu	No
Auto off timers	Setup menu	No
Beep	Setup menu	No
Date imprint	Setup menu	No
Slot empty release lock	Setup menu	No
Movie settings	Setup menu	No
HDMI	Setup menu	No
Flicker reduction	Setup menu	No

Set up menu

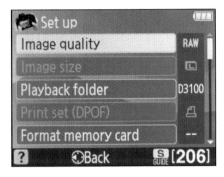

GUIDE MODE

Guide Mode (Easy operation) will quickly take you to the Close-up Scene Mode.

ISO: 500 *Focal Length:* 50mm
Shutter Speed: 1/640 sec. *Aperture:* f/5.6

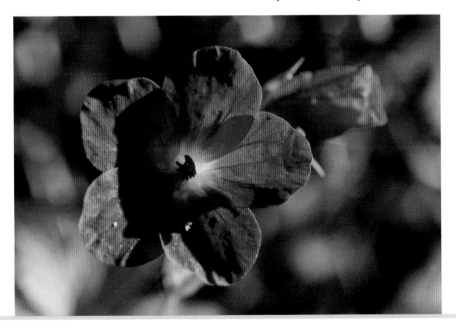

The D3100's large, bright LCD screen makes image playback a pleasure, and it's also highly informative. At the default settings, the most recent image is automatically displayed immediately after shooting, as well as whenever ▶ is pressed. If **Image review** is set to **Off** in the Playback menu, images are not automatically displayed. When Continuous release mode is in use, playback only begins after the last image in a burst has been captured, after which the pictures are shown in sequence.

Viewing additional pictures

To view the images on your memory card, other than the one most recently taken, scroll through them using the multi-selector. Scroll right to view images in the order of capture, or scroll left to view them in reverse order ("go back in time"). Various transition effects between one image and the next can be chosen from the Playback menu under **Display mode**, followed by **Transition effects**.

Viewing photo information

The D3100 records masses of information (*metadata*) about each image you take, and this can also be viewed on playback by using the multi-selector to scroll up or down through up to six pages of information. To make the following pages

available, go to the Playback menu and select **Display mode**. To make three detailed pages of shooting data available, ensure that **Data** is checked. To make the Highlights display available, select check **Highlights**, and to make the RGB histogram display available, check **RGB histogram**. To make any changes effective you must scroll up to **Done** and press the (OK) button.

If these options are unchecked, just two pages are available—a full-screen view of the image and an overview page that includes basic shooting information and a simplified histogram.

Highlights

The Highlights screen displays a flashing warning for any areas of the image that are completely white, where no detail has been recorded. This is one way to check that an image is correctly exposed and you haven't got any burnt-out highlights, and is certainly more objective than relying solely on a general impression of the image on the rear LCD screen.

AVOIDING CLIPPED HIGHLIGHTS »

I wanted this image to have some sparkle, but not to lose detail through clipped highlights, so I checked the highlight display after the first shot.

ISO: 200 *Focal Length:* 24mm
Shutter Speed: 1/200 sec. *Aperture:* f/13

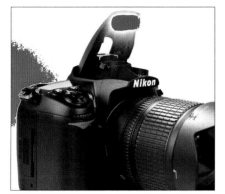

THE HIGHLIGHTS DISPLAY »

This image is taken from Adobe Lightroom, and the clipped highlights are shown in red. In the display on the camera's rear LCD screen, these areas would flash black.

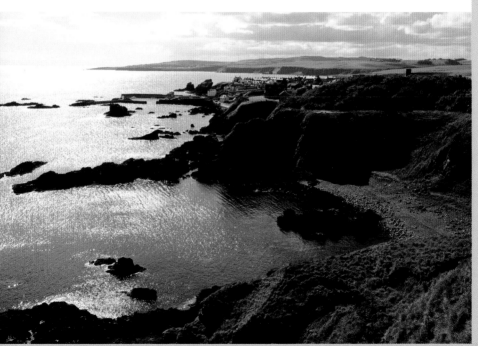

Histogram displays

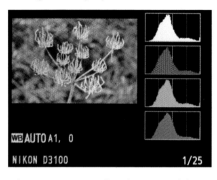

A histogram is a graphic depiction of the distribution of dark and light tones in an image. As a way of assessing if an image is correctly exposed it's far more precise than just looking at the full-frame playback, especially in bright sunlight when it can be difficult to see the screen image clearly. A single histogram is always available during playback, but selecting **Playback mode** in the **Playback menu** and checking **RGB histogram** gives you access to a more detailed display that shows individual histograms for the three color channels (red, green, and blue). The histogram display is the single most useful feature of image playback and it's normally the first thing I look at. Learning to interpret the histogram is a massive help in getting the best results from your D3100.

Playback zoom

To assess sharpness, or for other critical viewing, it is possible to zoom in on a section of an image. For Large images (including RAW files) the maximum magnification is approximately 27x.

1) Press ⊕ to zoom in on the image currently displayed. Press ⊕ repeatedly to increase the magnification and press ⊖▣ to zoom out again. When you are zoomed in, a small navigation window appears, with a yellow outline indicating the area currently visible in the monitor.

2) Use the multi-selector to view other areas of the image.

3) Rotate the Command Dial to view corresponding areas of other images at the same magnification.

Tip

The camera can detect up to 35 faces in an image during playback zoom; any faces detected are outlined in white in the navigation window. Press ◀🔢▶ and use ▲ or ▼ to zoom in or out on a selected face. Press ◀🔢▶ and use ◀ or ▶ to move between faces.

4) To return to full-frame viewing, press the ⊙K button, or exit playback completely by pressing ▶ or the shutter-release button.

Viewing images as thumbnails

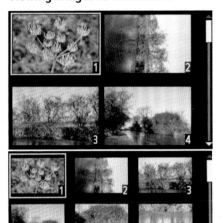

To view more than one image at once, press ⊖▦ once to display four images, again for nine images, and a third time to show 72 thumbnail images on screen. Use the multi-selector to scroll through the images—the currently selected image is outlined in yellow. To return to the full-frame view, press ⊙K.

Calendar View

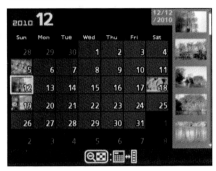

Calendar View displays images grouped by the date they were taken. Having pressed ⊖▦ three times to display 72 thumbnail images, press it once more to reach the first calendar page (date view), with the most recent date highlighted, and pictures taken on that date appearing in a vertical strip to the right. In this view, the multi-selector can be used to navigate to different dates.

If you press ⊖▦ again, you highlight the thumbnail list for the selected date and can then scroll through pictures taken on that day. Press ⊕ to see a larger preview of the currently selected image or press ⊖▦ to go back to date view.

In date view, if you press ⊕ you can return through the 72, nine, and four thumbnail screens to the full-frame view. Pressing ⊙K at any point will also return you to the full-frame view.

Deleting images

To delete the current image, or the selected image in thumbnail view, press 🗑. A confirmation dialog appears and to proceed with deletion you need to press 🗑 again. To cancel, press ▶.

In Calendar View (date view) you can also delete all images taken on a selected date. Again, press 🗑 and when the confirmation dialog appears press 🗑 again to delete or ▶ to cancel.

Protecting images

To protect the current image—or the selected image in thumbnail view/calendar view—against accidental deletion, press *AE-L/AF-L*. Press *AE-L/AF-L* again to remove its protection.

Warning!

Protected images will be deleted when the memory card is formatted.

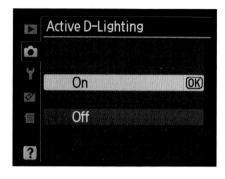

The D3100 allows you to adjust and enhance your images in a variety of ways, in camera. These adjustment options divide into two: settings that can be applied to an image before shooting and affect how the camera processes the image, and changes that can be made to pictures that are already on the memory card, creating a retouched copy.

Adjustments that can be applied to images already on the memory card are gathered in the Retouch Menu, but it is worth noting that the similarly named Active D-Lighting (applied pre-shoot) and D-Lighting (applied post-shoot using the Retouch menu) are different.

Pre-shoot controls

Many user-controlled settings affect the qualities of the final image, whether it's the exposure, the white balance, or something else, but the D3100 has yet more options that can alter the look of the picture. The two main ones are Nikon Picture Controls and Active D-Lighting, which can only be accessed when shooting in **P**, **A**, **S**, or **M** modes. In the Full Auto and Scene Modes, Active D-Lighting is switched off and the Picture Controls are pre-set.

Active-D Lighting

Active D-Lighting is designed to enhance the D3100's ability to cope with scenes that show a wide range of brightness (*dynamic range*). In simple terms, it reduces the overall exposure in order to capture more detail in the brightest areas, while midtone and shadow areas are lightened as the camera processes the image, to prevent an underexposed result.

1) In the Active Information Display, select **ADL** and press (OK). Alternatively, in the Shooting menu, select **Active D-Lighting**.

2) Select **Off** or **On** and press (OK).

> **Note:**
> *These settings are useful for improving the quality of JPEG images, but if you are shooting RAW files they have no effect on the data.*

ACTIVE D-LIGHTING ≫
With bright sunlight ahead, but deep shadows in the foreground, contrast was very high: just the sort of situation where Active D-Lighting is needed.

ISO: 400 *Focal Length:* 35mm
Shutter Speed: 1/40 sec. *Aperture:* f/5.6

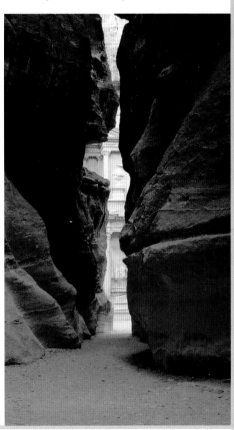

2 › Picture controls

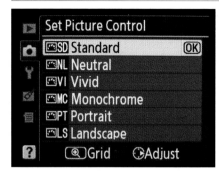

Picture Controls influence the way in which JPEG files are processed by the camera. In all modes the current Picture Control is indicated toward the top center of the Information Display. In Full Auto and Scene Modes the Picture Control is predetermined, but when shooting in **P**, **A**, **S**, or **M** modes you have a free hand to choose and fine-tune them.

The D3100 offers a choice of six preset Picture Controls. Names such as Neutral (**NL**) and Vivid (**VI**) are self-explanatory, and Monochrome (**MC**) even more so. Standard (**SD**) gives a compromise setting that works well in a wide range of situations. Portrait (**PT**) is designed to deliver slightly lower contrast and saturation, with a color balance that is flattering to skin-tones, while Landscape (**LS**) produces higher contrast and saturation for more vibrant images.

Selecting Nikon Picture Controls

1) In the Shooting menu, select **Set Picture Control**.

2) Use the multi-selector to highlight the required Picture Control and press (OK). This Picture Control will apply to all images taken in **P**, **A**, **S**, or **M** modes until the setting is changed. Scene Modes apply preset Picture Controls.

Modifying Picture Controls

The standard Nikon Picture Controls can be modified, by using either **Quick Adjust** to make swift global changes, or manual adjustments to specific parameters.

1) From the Shooting menu, select **Set Picture Control**.

2) Use the Multi-Selector to highlight the required Picture Control and press ▶.

3) Scroll up or down with the Multi Selector to select **Quick Adjust** or one of the specific parameters. Use ▶ or ◀ to change the value as desired.

4) When all parameters are as required, press (OK). The new values are retained (for images taken in **P**, **A**, **S**, or **M** modes) until that Picture Control is modified again, or you reset the shooting options.

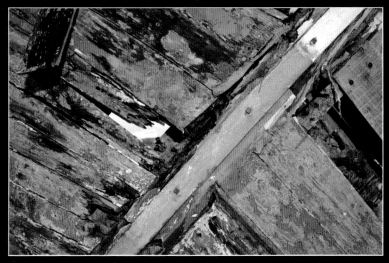

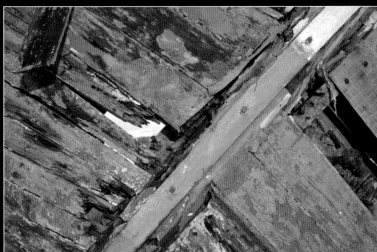

PICTURE CONTROLS ⨪
Two otherwise identical images with Vivid (*top*)
and Neutral (*bottom*) Picture Controls applied.

2 » USING THE D3100 MENUS

The options that you can access through buttons, the Command Dial, and the Active Information Display are only the tip of the iceberg, and the true extent to which the D3100 can be customized to suit your particular shooting needs is only revealed by delving into its menus. There are five of these: Playback, Shooting, Setup, Retouch, and Recent Settings. The menu screen also shows a ? icon but there isn't a separate Help menu as such. Instead, you access help from within the other menus by pressing the **?** button. The advantage of this is the help is contextual, so it provides an explanation that is relevant to the menu or setting that is currently on screen.

The Playback menu is underlined in blue and used to control functions related to playback, including viewing, naming, or deleting images.

The Shooting menu is underlined in green and used to control shooting settings, such as ISO speed or White Balance (also accessible via the Active Information Display), as well as Picture Controls and Active D-Lighting.

The Setup menu is underlined in orange and used for functions such as LCD brightness, plus others that you may rarely access, such as language and time settings.

The Retouch menu, underlined in purple, is used to create modified copies of images already on the memory card.

Finally, Recent Settings is underlined in gray and allows fast access to recently used items from any of the other menus.

Navigating the menus

1) To display the main menu screen, press **MENU**.

2) Use ▲ or ▼ to highlight the main menus along the left of the screen, and ▶ or (OK) to open it.

3) Use ▲ or ▼ to highlight the various menu items. To select a particular item press ▶ or (OK). This will take you to a further set of options.

4) Using ▲ or ▼, scroll to the desired setting and press ▶ or (OK). In some cases it's necessary to select **DONE** and then press (OK) to make the changes effective.

5) To return to the previous screen, press ◀. To exit the menus completely, without making any changes, semi-depress the shutter-release button.

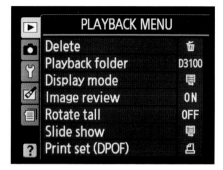

The D3100's Playback Menu contains options that affect how images are viewed, stored, deleted, and printed. It is only accessible when a memory card is present in the camera.

Delete

This function allows images stored on the memory card to be deleted, either singly or in batches.

1) In the Playback menu, highlight **Delete** and press ▶.

2) In the menu options screen, choose **Selected**. Images in the active playback folder are displayed as thumbnail images.

3) Use the multi-selector to scroll through the displayed images. Press and hold ⊕ to view the highlighted image full-screen. Press ⊖💥 to mark the highlighted shot for deletion. It will be tagged with a 🗑. If

you change your mind, highlight a tagged image and press ⊖💥 to remove the tag.

4) Repeat this procedure to select further images or, to exit without deleting any pictures, press **MENU** .

5) Press ⑥ to see a confirmation screen. Select **YES** and press ⑥ to delete the selected image(s). To exit without deleting any images, select **NO**.

> *Note:*
> *Individual images can also be deleted when using the playback screen by pressing the 🗑 button. This is usually quicker than the Playback menu.*

Select date

Allows deletion of all images taken on a selected date.

1) In the Playback menu, highlight **Delete** and press ▶.

2) Choose **Select date** from the menu options and press ▶. A list of dates appears (corresponding to images on the memory card), with a sample image shown for each date. Use ▲ or ▼ to scroll to your desired date and press ▶ to select it.

1) In the Playback menu, highlight **Delete** and press ▶.

2) Choose **Select date** from the menu options and press ▶. A list of dates appears (corresponding to images on the memory card), with a sample image shown for each date. Use ▲ or ▼ to scroll to your desired date and press ▶ to select it.

3) Press (OK) to delete all the images taken on that date, or, to review those images, press ⊖🔳 to see a screen of thumbnails. You can navigate through these in the usual way with the multi-selector and press ⊕ to see an image full-screen, but you can't zoom in. Press ⊖🔳 to return to the date-selection screen.

4) With one or more dates checked, press (OK) to see a confirmation screen. Select YES and press (OK) to delete all image(s). To exit without deleting, select NO.

Delete All:

1) To delete all images on a card, highlight **Delete** and press ▶.

2) In the menu options screen, choose **All**.

3) Press (OK) to see a confirmation screen. Select **YES** and press (OK) to delete all image(s), or choose **NO** to exit without deleting any pictures.

> **Note:**
> The current folder is chosen through the Setup menu (see page 103).

Playback folder

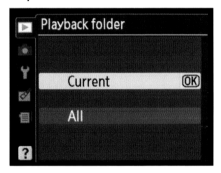

By default, the D3100's playback screen only displays images in the current folder. If multiple folders exist on the memory card, images in other folders will not be visible. If a memory card is inserted

PLAYBACK FOLDER OPTIONS	
Current (default)	Displays images in the current folder only.
All	Displays images in all folders on the memory card.

containing images from a different model of camera (even another Nikon DSLR) they will not be visible on the D3100, but you can change this.

Display mode

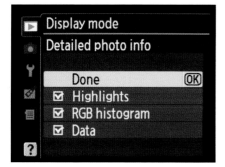

This is an important menu, enabling you to choose what (if any) information about each image will be displayed on playback, over and above the basic info screen that is always available.

Image review

If Image review is **ON**, images are automatically displayed on the monitor immediately after shooting. If set to **OFF** they can only be displayed by pressing **?**.

Rotate tall

This enables you to determine whether portrait format ("tall") images will be displayed "right way up" during playback. If set to **OFF**, which is the default, these images will not be rotated, meaning that you need to turn the camera through 90° to view them correctly. If set to **ON**, these images will be displayed right way up, but

DISPLAY MODE OPTIONS		
	Highlights	Areas of "blown" highlights are shown as black blinking areas in full-screen playback.
Detailed photo info	RGB histogram	Makes a separate playback page available, with histograms for the three individual color channels.
	Data	Makes three further playback pages available, containing detailed information about the image.

because the screen is rectangular, they will appear smaller. **ON** is mainly useful when displaying images on a television.

Slide show

Enables you to display images as a standard slide show on the camera's own screen or through a television. All the images in the folder or folders selected for playback (under the Playback Folder menu) will be played in chronological order.

1) In the Playback menu, select **Slide show**.

2) Select **Frame interval** and choose between intervals of 2, 3, 5, or 10 seconds. Press OK to confirm your choice.

3) Choose **Transition effects** to change the appearance of the transition between slides. The options are **Zoom/fade, Cube,** and **None**.

4) Select Start and press OK.

5) When the show ends, a dialog screen is displayed. Select **Restart** and press OK to play again, or choose **Frame interval** and press OK to return to the Frame interval dialog. Select **Exit** and press OK to exit.

6) If you press OK during the slide show, the slide show is paused. If you select

Restart and press OK, the show will resume where it left off.

7) To skip ahead, or skip back, while a slide show is playing, press ▶ or ◀ respectively.

8) To change the display mode during a slide show (to see a histogram for each image, for example), press ▲ or ▼.

Print set (DPOF)

This allows you to select image(s) to be printed when the camera is connected to a printer that complies with the **DPOF** (Digital Print Order Format) standard. **DPOF** print orders can also be saved on the memory card for later use—at a photographic printing outlet, for example.

> **Note:**
>
> *Only JPEG images can be set using Print set (DPOF), not NEF (RAW) files.*

› The Shooting menu

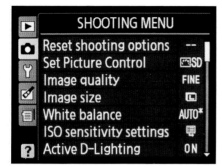

The Shooting menu contains numerous options, but many of these are also accessible through the Active Information Display. As they have already been discussed, they can be covered briefly here.

Reset shooting options
Resets most options to their default settings.

Set Picture Control
Only available in **P**, **A**, **S**, and **M** exposure modes, this menu sets the desired Nikon Picture Control.

> **Note:**
> If the image quality is set to RAW, or RAW+FINE, Set Picture Control is grayed out and cannot be accessed.

Image quality
Choose between RAW and JPEG files.

Image size
Use this to choose between Small, Medium, and Large JPEG image sizes.

White balance
Allows you to set the White Balance in **P**, **A**, **S**, and **M** exposure modes.

ISO sensitivity settings
Sets the ISO sensitivity setting.

Active D-Lighting
Activates or disables Active D-Lighting in **P**, **A**, **S**, and **M** exposure modes.

Auto distortion control
If **ON**, this automatically corrects the distortion that may arise with certain lenses. Recommended only for Type G and Type D lenses, excluding fisheye and perspective control (PC) lenses. Only affects JPEG images, not NEF (RAW) files.

Color space
Allows you to choose between the sRGB and Adobe RGB color space.

2

Noise reduction

Photos taken at long shutter speeds and/or high ISO sensitivity settings can be subject to increased "noise," so the D3100 offers the option of additional image processing to counteract this. If noise reduction is **ON**, it applies to images taken at ISO settings over ISO 800 and/or exposure times of 8 seconds or longer.

When long exposure noise reduction is applied the image processing takes roughly the same amount of time as the shutter speed being used, so a 10-second exposure time would require approximately 10 seconds of processing. During this time, **Job nr** appears, blinking, in the viewfinder, and no further pictures can be taken until the processing is complete. This can cause significant delays in shooting so it may be preferable to remove image noise during post-processing instead. Because of this, the default setting is **OFF**, although a limited degree of noise reduction will still be applied to JPEG images shot at above ISO 1600.

AF-area mode

Selects the AF-area mode, although this is more usually chosen through the Active Information Display.

Metering

Allows you to select the metering pattern. Again, this is more usually chosen through the Active Information Display.

Movie settings

Sets key options for shooting movies.

Built-in flash

Determines whether the output of the built-in flash is controlled automatically (**TTL**) or manually (**Manual**). Selecting Manual brings up a sub-menu that allows the strength of the flash output to be set.

› The Setup menu

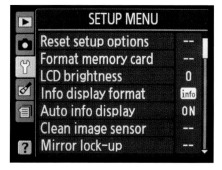

The Setup menu allows access to a number of important camera functions, although many will only be accessed occasionally.

Reset setup options
Resets most options in this menu to their default settings.

Format memory card
The one item in this menu that most users will employ regularly.

LCD brightness
Allows the brightness of the rear LCD screen to be adjusted to suit the ambient lighting conditions.

Info display format
Switches between two display modes for the Information Display: **Graphic** (default) and **Classic**. You can also select different background colors for each display mode.

Auto info display
Determines whether the Information Display appears automatically when the shutter-release button is half-pressed. It can also be displayed straight after a shot is taken, but only if Image Review is **Off**. There are different options for **P**, **A**, **S**, or **M** modes and for Auto/Scene modes, as you may refer to the Information Display far more when working with the User-control modes.

Clean image sensor
Strictly speaking, it is not the sensor, but the protective low-pass filter in front of it that can attract dust and require cleaning. The D3100 has an automated procedure to do this, which vibrates the low-pass filter at various frequencies. Experience suggests that this is highly effective and greatly reduces both the incidence of dust spots on images and the need for more invasive

> **Note:**
> *It is suggested that cleaning is most effective if the camera is placed base-down at the time, which may not be the case if you are in the habit of switching the camera on/off while you're stowing it in a bag, or taking it out.*

forms of cleaning. The Clean image sensor menu allows you to actuate cleaning at any time, as well as setting the camera to clean automatically at startup and/or shutdown.

Video mode

This is not directly related to the camera's movie mode, but sets the camera to either the PAL or NTSC standard if you want to view your images on a television. NTSC is used in North America and Japan, while PAL is used in most of the rest of the world.

HDMI

You can connect the D3100 to HDMI (High Definition Multimedia Interface) television, but you'll need a special cable. This menu sets the camera's output to match the HDMI device (get this information from that device's specs or instructions). When connected to an HDMI-CEC television, you can use the Device control submenu to allow the television's remote control to be used to navigate through the images stored on the memory card.

Mirror lock-up

Allows access to the low-pass filter for manual cleaning.

Flicker reduction

Some light sources can produce a visible flicker in the Live View screen image and during movie recording. To minimize this, use this menu to match the frequency of the local mains power supply: 60Hz is common in North America, while 50Hz is normal in the European Union, including the UK.

Time zone and date

Allows you to set the date, time, and time zone, and to specify the format in which the date is displayed (Y/M/D, M/D/Y or D/M/Y). It's best to start by setting the time zone in which you normally operate, before setting the time. If you travel to a different time zone, you then need only change the time zone and the time will be corrected automatically.

Language

Sets the language used for the camera menus. The options include most major European languages, plus Arabic, Chinese, Japanese, Korean, Indonesian, and Thai.

Image comment

Allows you to add text comments to images as they are shot. Comments appear in the third page of the photo info display (when this is activated using **Display mode** in the Playback Menu) and can also be viewed in Nikon View NX2 and Nikon Capture NX2.

The process of text input is similar to

text messaging on a mobile phone. To input a comment, select **Input comment** and press (**OK**). Use the multi-selector to move through the available characters, and press (**OK**) to use the highlighted character. Use the Command Dial to move the cursor forward or back in the text. When you are finished, press ⊕. Select **Attach comment**, then Done, and press (**OK**). The comment will be attached to all subsequent shots until turned off.

Auto image rotation

If set to **ON** (default), information about the orientation of the camera is recorded with each photo taken, so they will appear the right way up when viewed with *Nikon View NX2, Nikon Capture NX2*, or most third-party imaging applications. Exceptions can occur if shots are taken with the camera pointing steeply up or down, or when panning; in these cases orientation data may not be recorded. It may be worth setting Auto image rotation to **OFF** if a sequence of such shots is planned, but in practice there is little to be gained by doing this.

Dust Off ref photo

Nikon Capture NX2 software (not supplied with the D3100) features automatic dust removal by comparing your images with a reference shot that maps the dust on the

sensor. If there are stubborn dust spots that won't succumb to normal sensor cleaning, then using a dust-off reference shot can save a lot of retouching work.

To take a dust-off reference photo

1) Fit a CPU lens of at least 50mm focal length. If it's a zoom, use the longest focal length. Locate a bright, featureless white object—such as a sheet of plain paper—that is large enough to fill the frame.

2) In the Setup menu, select **Dust off ref photo** and press (**OK**).

3) Select **Start** or **Clean sensor** and then **Start** and press (**OK**). (Do not select **Clean sensor** and then **Start** if the pictures from which spots are to be removed have already been taken).

4) When the camera is ready to shoot the reference photo, **rEF** will appear in the viewfinder.

5) Frame the white object at a distance of approximately 4 inches/10 cm. Press the shutter-release button halfway.

6) Press the shutter-release button fully to complete the process. If the reference object is too bright or dark, a warning will be displayed, so change the exposure settings or choose another reference object and re-shoot.

Auto off timers

Governs the interval before the information, playback, and viewfinder displays turn off if no further actions are carried out.

Short, Normal, and Long determine standard times for each of the three displays, with a short delay best if you want to preserve your battery,

Custom allows you to set the timings for each display individually. The meters will not turn off automatically when the D3100 is connected to a mains adaptor.

Self-timer delay

Allows you to set the delay in self-timer-release mode before the shutter fires. The options are 10 seconds or 2 seconds.

Beep

Determines whether a beep sounds when the self-timer operates or to signify that focus has been acquired when shooting in Single-servo AF mode. Options are simply On or Off.

Rangefinder

If this option is set to On, the electronic rangefinder is available to assist with manual focusing.

File number sequence

This item controls the way file numbers are set. Switched Off, file numbering is reset to 0001 whenever a new memory card is inserted, the card is formatted, or a new folder is created. If On, numbering continues sequentially from the previous highest number used. Reset means that 1 is added to the largest number used in the current folder. If you only use one image folder, then On and Reset are effectively the same.

Buttons

This menu item has three sub-sections that allow you to change the functions of three of the camera's control buttons as outlined in the table *right*.

Slot empty release lock

This menu item has two options. When Release locked (default) is selected, pictures cannot be taken unless a memory card is inserted in the camera. If Enable release is selected, the shutter can be released even if no memory card is present. Images are held in the camera's buffer and can be displayed on the monitor, but are not recorded.

Date imprint

Determines whether the date and time are imprinted on photographs as they are taken. The default setting is Off. Other options allow the imprint of Date, Date

and time, or **Date counter**, which imprints the number of days to/from a selected date. Imprint applies to JPEG photos only.

Storage folder

By default, the D3100 stores images in a single folder (named 100D3100). If multiple memory cards are used they will all end up holding folders of the same name. This isn't usually a problem, but a few users might wish to avoid it. You might also want to create specific folders for different shoots or different types of image.

Generally, it's organizing images on the computer that counts, but having separate folders in the camera sometimes helps.

SECTION	OPTIONS
Fn	**Image quality/size:** Press button and rotate Command Dial to scroll through a full range of image quality/size options.
	ISO sensitivity: Press button and rotate command dial to select ISO setting.
	White balance (**P**, **A**, **S**, or **M** modes only): Press button and rotate Command Dial to select White Balance setting.
	Active D-Lighting (**P**, **A**, **S**, or **M** modes only): Press button and rotate Command Dial to turn ADL On or Off.
AE-L/AF-L	**AE/AF lock** (default): Press and hold button to lock focus and exposure.
	AE lock only: Press and hold button to lock exposure.
	AF lock only: Press and hold button to lock focus.
	AE lock (hold): Press button to lock exposure.
	AF-ON: When AF-ON is selected, only the AE-L/AF-L button (not the shutter-release button) can be used to initiate autofocus.
AE-L	**On:** Half-pressure on the shutter-release button locks both exposure and focus.
	Off (default): Half-pressure on the shutter-release button locks the focus only.

New folders are also created if an existing folder becomes full. "Full" is defined as containing 999 photos, irrespective of image quality or size. If you regularly copy images to your computer and then format the memory card (which is recommended), the folder may never reach this capacity. However, a new folder will also be created when the total number of pictures taken reaches 9999, and it is certainly possible to take more than 10,000 photographs in the lifetime of a Nikon D3100.

In naming folders, you can't just use any name you like: only the last five digits of the name are editable. (In fact the first three digits are hidden when you use this menu, but the full name appears when the camera is connected to a computer).

To create a new folder

1) In the Shooting menu, select **Active folder** and press (OK).

2) Select New and press (OK).

3) A screen of letters and numbers appears. Enter a new name.

4) Press ⊕ to create the new folder and return to the Shooting menu. It automatically becomes the active folder. You can also rename an existing folder: at

step 2 above, select **Rename** and press (OK). The procedure is then similar.

To change the active folder

This assumes that more than one folder already exists on the memory card.

1) In the Shooting menu, select **Storage folder** and press (OK).

2) Choose **Select folder** and press (OK).

3) Scroll up or down the folder list. To select the highlighted folder press (OK). To exit without making a change, press **MENU**.

GPS

Used when the D3100 is connected to a compatible GPS device.

Firmware version

Firmware is the onboard software that controls the camera's operation. Nikon issues updates periodically. This menu displays the firmware version currently installed in the camera, enabling users to ascertain whether their camera has the current firmware. When new firmware is released, it must first be downloaded from the Nikon website and then copied to a memory card. Insert this card in the camera and use this menu to update the camera's firmware.

› The Retouch menu

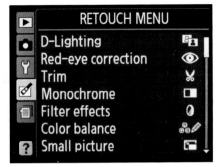

FORMAT OF ORIGINAL PHOTO	QUALITY AND SIZE OF COPY
NEF (RAW)	Fine, Large (JPEG)
JPEG	Quality and size match original

The Retouch Menu is used to make a variety of corrections and enhancements to images, including cropping, color balance, and more. It is important to note that retouching does not modify the original image in any way. Instead, it creates a copy to which the changes are applied. Further retouch options—up to a maximum of ten steps—can be applied to the new copy, but you can't apply the same effect twice to the same image. Copies are always created in JPEG format but the size and quality of the copy depends on the format of the original, as outlined in the table below. Exceptions are options such as **Trim** and **Small Picture**, which produce smaller copies.

There are two ways to access the retouch options and create a copy: the steps of the process are basically the same, but in a slightly different order.

From the Image Playback screen

1) Display the image you wish to retouch.

2) Press (OK) and the Retouch menu appears over the image.

3) Select the desired retouch option and press ▶. If subsidiary options open, make a further selection and press ▶ again. A preview of the retouched image will be shown on the LCD screen.

4) Depending on the type of retouching to be done, there may be further options to choose from.

5) Press (OK) to create a retouched copy. The access lamp will blink briefly as the copy is created. ◀ takes you back to the options screen and ▶ or **MENU** exits without creating the copy.

› Retouch menu options

From the Retouch menu

1) In the Retouch menu, select the desired retouch option and press ▶. If subsidiary options are offered, make a further selection and press ▶ again. A screen of image thumbnails appears.

2) Select the required image using the multi-selector, as you would during regular image playback, and then press (OK). A preview of the retouched image appears.

3) Depending on the type of retouching to be done, there may be further options to choose from.

4) Press (OK) to create a retouched copy. The access lamp will blink briefly as the copy is created. ◀ takes you back to the options screen and ▶ or **MENU** exits without creating the copy.

> **Note:**
> A ✎ icon in normal image playback indicates retouched copy images.

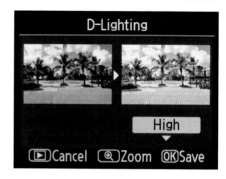

D-Lighting

D-Lighting should not be confused with Active D-Lighting, although the end result is similar. The key difference is that Active D-Lighting is selected *before* shooting and affects the way the original image is exposed and processed, whereas D-Lighting is applied *after* shooting and creates a retouched copy. Both effects aim to deal with high-contrast subjects and their primary effect is to lighten the shadow areas of the image. However, because it affects the original image exposure, Active D-Lighting is better at dealing with overly bright highlights. The D-Lighting screen shows a side-by-side comparison of the original image and the retouched version; a press on ⊕ zooms in on the retouched version. Use ▲ and ▼ to select the strength of the effect—**High**, **Normal**, or **Low**.

Red-eye correction

This is aimed at the notorious problem of "red-eye," which is commonly caused by on-camera flash. As a result, this option can only be selected for images that were taken using flash. The camera analyzes the photo for evidence of red-eye. If no red-eye is found, the process will go no further, but if the camera detects red-eye in your picture a preview image will open and you can use the multi-selector and the zoom controls to view it more closely. If you've used the zoom, a first press on (OK) returns to full-screen view and a second press on (OK) creates a retouched copy.

Trim

This allows you to crop an image to eliminate unwanted areas or to fit it better to a specific print size. When this option is selected, a preview screen appears, with the crop area shown by a yellow rectangle.

Change the aspect ratio of the crop by rotating the command dial: choose from 3:2 (the same as the original image), 4:3, 5:4, 1:1 (square) and 16:9. Adjust the size of the cropped area using the ⊖ and ⊕ buttons. Adjust its position using the multi-selector and press (OK) to save the cropped image as a copy.

Monochrome

This creates a monochrome copy of the original image. You can choose from straight Black-and-white, Sepia (a brownish, toned effect similar to many antique photos), and Cyanotype (a bluish-toned effect). If you select Sepia or Cyanotype, a preview screen appears that allows you to adjust the toning effect. To make it stronger or weaker use ▼ and ▲.

Filter effects

Mimics several common photographic

ASPECT RATIO	POSSIBLE SIZES FOR TRIMMED COPY (PIXELS)						
3:2	3840x2560	3200x2128	2560x1704	1920x1280	1280x856	960x640	640x424
4:3	3840x2880	3840x2400	2560x1920	1920x1440	1280x960	960x720	640x480
5:4	3600x2880	2992x2400	2400x1920	1808x1440	1200x960	896x720	608x480
1:1	2880x2880	2400x2400	1920x1920	1440x1440	960x960	720x720	480x480
16:9	3840x2160	3200x1800	2560x1440	1920x1080	1280x720	960x536	640x360

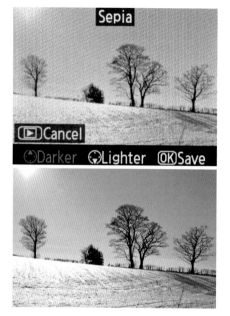

Applying a sepia effect in the Retouch menu, ⌃ and the resulting image

filters. **Skylight** reduces the blue cast that can affect photos taken on clear days with a lot of blue sky, but applied to other images its effect is very subtle, even undetectable. **Warm filter** has a much stronger warming effect. **Red**, **green**, and **blue intensifier** are all fairly self-explanatory, as is **Soft**, but **Cross screen** is less obvious. This creates a "starburst" effect around light sources and other very bright points (such as sparkling highlights on water), with multiple options available as shown in the table below.

Color balance

Creates a copy with modified color balance. When this option is selected, a preview screen appears and the multi-selector can be used to move a cursor around a color grid. The effect is shown both in the preview and in the histograms that accompany it.

CROSS SCREEN OPTIONS	OPTIONS AVAILABLE
Number of points	Create a 4-, 6-, or 8-pointed star.
Filter amount	Choose the brightness of light sources that are affected.
Filter angle	Choose angle of the star-points.
Length of points	Choose length of the star-points.
Confirm	See a preview of the effect; press ⊕ to see it full-screen.
Save	Create a copy incorporating the effect.

Small picture

This option creates a small copy of the selected picture(s), suitable for immediate use on a variety of devices, as well as for Websites and emailing. Three possible sizes are available, but even the largest of these is inadequate for devices such as Apple's iPad, so you may be better off using **Trim** instead (or simply don't bother—the iPad will display full-size photos beautifully).

Small picture can be accessed from the Retouch Menu or from Image playback, but there are slight differences in the procedure. If starting from the Retouch menu, you select a picture size first and then select the picture(s) to be copied at that size. If starting from Image playback, you select a picture first and then choose the size for the copy. Small pictures appear with a gray border in normal image playback and it is not possible to zoom in on them.

Image overlay

Image overlay allows you to create a new image that combines two existing pictures. This can only be applied to originals in NEF (RAW) format, but Nikon claims that the results are better than combining the images in an image manipulation program application such as Photoshop as Image overlay makes direct use of the raw data from the D3100's sensor.

> **Note:**
> Although Image overlay works from RAW images, the size and quality of the new image are not automatically set to JPEG Fine/Large as they are with other retouch options. This means it is possible to create a new RAW image, or create JPEG files of any size and quality. Before activating Image overlay make sure the Image Quality and Image Size options are set.

SMALL PICTURE SIZE	POSSIBLE USES
640 x 480 pixels	Display on standard (not HD) television. Also for hi-res smartphones such as Apple's iPhone.
320 x 240 pixels	Display on mid-range mobile devices.
160 x 120 pixels	Display on small-screen mobile devices such as cellphones.

To create an overlaid image

1) In the Retouch menu, select **Image overlay** and press (OK). A dialogue screen appears with sections labeled **Image 1**, **Image 2**, and **Preview**. Initially, **Image 1** is highlighted. Press (OK).

2) The camera displays thumbnails of all the RAW images on the memory card. Select the first image you want to use for the overlay and press (OK).

3) Select **Gain**: this determines how much "weight" this image has in the final overlay. Use ▲ and ▼ to adjust the gain from a default value of 1.0.

4) Press ▶ to move to **Image 2** and repeat steps 2 and 3 with your second RAW image.

5) If necessary, press ◀ to return to **Image 1** and make further adjustments to the gain, or even press (OK) to change the selected image.

6) Finally, press ▶ to highlight **Preview**. Select **Overlay** and press (OK) to preview the result. If you are not satisfied you can return to the previous stage by pressing ⊖⊞. If you are satisfied with your overlaid image, press (OK) again and the new file will be created. You can also skip the preview stage by highlighting **Save** and pressing (OK).

NEF (RAW) Processing

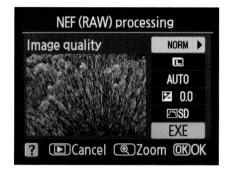

This menu creates a JPEG copy from an image that was originally shot as a RAW file. While this is no substitute for full RAW processing on a computer, it does allow the creation of quick copies for immediate sharing or printing. Options available for the processing of RAW images are displayed in a column to the right of the preview image (see table *opposite*) and these provide a reasonable level of control over the conversion process.

When you are satisfied with the preview image select **EXE** and press (OK) to create the JPEG copy. Pressing ▶ or **MENU** exits the menu without creating a copy.

Quick retouch

Provides basic one-step retouching for a quick fix, boosting saturation and contrast.

NEF (RAW) PROCESSING OPTIONS	DESCRIPTION
Image quality	Choose Fine, Normal, or Basic JPEG.
Filter amount	Choose Large, Medium, or Small image size.
White balance	Choose a white balance setting.
Exposure comp.	Adjust exposure level from +3EV to -3EV.
Set Picture Control	Choose any of the range of Nikon Picture Controls to be applied to the image.

D-Lighting is applied automatically to retain shadow detail. Use ▲ and ▼ to increase or reduce the strength of the effect, then press (OK) to create the retouched copy.

Straighten
It's best to get horizons level at the time of shooting, but it doesn't always happen. This option allows correction of up to 5° in steps of 0.25°. Use ▶ to rotate clockwise and ◀ to rotate counterclockwise. Inevitably, this crops the image slightly. Press (OK) to create the retouched copy or ▶ to exit without creating a copy.

Distortion control
Some lenses create noticeable curvature of straight lines. Distortion control allows you to correct this in-camera, although it will crop your image slightly. **Auto** allows automatic compensation for the known

characteristics of Type G and Type D Nikkor lenses, so it can't be used on images taken with other lenses. **Manual** can be applied whatever lens was used; use ▶ to reduce barrel distortion or ◀ to reduce pincushion distortion. The multi-selector can also be used to fine-tune an image after the **Auto** control has been applied.

Fisheye
This is almost the reverse of the previous effect, applying exaggerated barrel distortion to give a fisheye lens effect. Use ▶ to strengthen the effect and ◀ to reduce it.

Color outline
This detects edges in the photograph and uses them to create a "line-drawing" effect. This could be used as a starting point for a painting or illustration, either by hand or using illustration software. There are no

options for fine-tuning the effect in-camera.

Perspective control

Corrects the convergence of vertical lines in photos taken looking up at tall buildings, for example. Grid lines aid in assessing the distortion, and the strength of the correction is controlled with the multi-selector. The process inevitably crops the original image, so it is vital to leave space around the subject.

Miniature effect

This option mimics the in-vogue technique for shooting images with an extremely small and localized depth of field, making real landscapes or city views look more like miniature models. It usually works best with photos taken from a high viewpoint, which typically have clearer separation between the foreground and background. A yellow rectangle shows the area that will remain in sharp focus, which can be repositioned using the multi-selector. Press ⊕ to preview the result, and press (OK) to save a retouched copy.

Edit movie

This item has a rather inflated title given that it only allows you to trim the start and/

or end of a movie clip. Yet while it's a very long way from proper movie-editing, it may have its uses when a clip is required straight away.

To trim a movie clip:

1) Select a movie clip in full-frame playback. Press (OK) to play the movie.

2) Press ▼ to pause. If this is the point at which you want to trim the movie, proceed to the next step. Otherwise press (OK) to resume playback or ◀ to rewind.

3) Press *AE-L/AF-L* to display the **Edit movie** options.

4) Select **Choose start point** or **Choose end point** as appropriate and press (OK) to trim the clip at this point.

5) Repeat if necessary to trim the other end of the clip.

6) Select **Yes** and press (OK) to save the trimmed clip as a copy. Note that the original is retained.

> **Note:**
> At Step 4 you also have an option to **Save selected frame**, which creates a JPEG image from the selected movie frame.

Before and After

Although it relates to retouched images, you can't access this option from the Retouch menu, only from full-frame playback. It is also only available when a retouched copy—or an image that was used as the source of a retouched copy—is selected.

With a suitable image selected, press $\textcircled{OK}$ then select **Before and After** from the listed options and press $\textcircled{OK}$ again to display the retouched copy alongside the original source image.

Highlight either image with ◀ or ▶ and press and hold $\oplus$ to view it full frame. Press ▶ to return to normal playback or press $\textcircled{OK}$ to return to the playback screen with the highlighted image selected.

› Recent Settings menu

The Recent Settings menu automatically stores the most recent settings (up to 20 items) made using any of the other menus, and provides a quick way to access controls that you have used recently. It is possible to delete items from the list, which can be useful if you've recently made extensive use of the Retouch menu, for example. By deleting the Retouch options, you bring shooting settings—which are usually more useful—back to the top of the list.

To remove items from the Recent Settings menu:

1) Highlight any item in the list and press 🗑 to select it for deletion. A confirmation dialog appears.

2) To go ahead with the deletion(s) press 🗑 again. To exit without deleting any of your settings, press **MENU**.

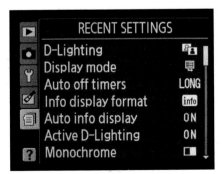

> **Note:**
> If you start with a "full" Recent Settings menu containing 20 items, deleting items simply makes the list shorter: the D3100 does not "recall" older items.

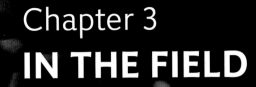

Chapter 3
IN THE FIELD

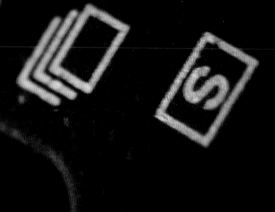

IN THE FIELD

Cameras such as the D3100 are so capable when it comes to taking pictures that getting the focus and exposure right is now rarely a major concern. However, there's a big difference between photos that "come out" and those that turn out exactly the way you want them.

Possessing a good camera does not guarantee stunning shots every time and photography still—thank goodness—offers ample scope for individual expression, vision, and skill.

Knowing what you want to achieve with any photograph is the real secret of success, no matter what camera you use, so the clearer your vision of what you want the picture to say, and how you want it to look, the better. If you know why you're taking the shot and what you want it to

show (and, just as important, what you want to leave out), then the "how" part will flow much more naturally.

Of course "how" is the main concern of this book—vision is a personal thing. Understanding the way in which light works, and how lenses and digital images behave, all makes it easier to take charge and realize your own, personal vision. However, the D3100 does not force you to dive in at the deep end and master all of these things at once.

Experimenting with Scene Modes shows how the camera can handle shooting opportunities in very different ways, but they are limited. Program (**P**) mode leaves the camera in charge of the key shooting parameters—aperture and shutter speed—while allowing you to make choices over other important settings such as White Balance, Picture Controls, or Active D-Lighting. Aperture Priority (**A**) and Shutter Priority (**S**) modes also give direct control over key settings, as well as the aperture or shutter speed, but they still allow the camera to determine correct exposure, while Manual (**M**) mode puts you in total control.

ESSENTIAL SKILLS ❯❯

Exposure, framing, and other skills are important, but there's still no substitute for being in the right place at the right time.

ISO: 160 *Focal Length:* 80mm
Shutter Speed: 1/1000 sec. *Aperture:* f/11

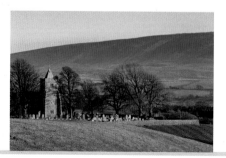

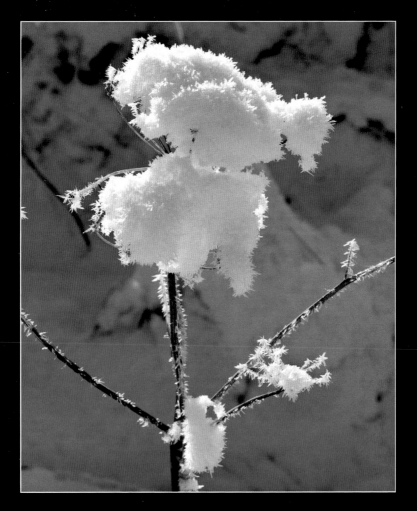

USING THE SPOTMETER ⌃

Most of this shot is shadow. I used spotmetering to try and ensure that the highlights did not burn out.

ISO: 125 ***Focal Length:*** 56mm
Shutter Speed: 1/250 sec. ***Aperture:*** f/11

3 » FOCUS AND DEPTH OF FIELD

No camera, no matter how sophisticated it is, always sees what the eye sees. Nothing illustrates this better than depth of field. In simple terms, depth of field means what's in focus and what isn't. A more precise definition is that *"depth of field is the zone, extending in front of and behind the point of focus, in which objects appear to be sharp in the final image."*

The human eye scans the world dynamically, so whatever we're looking at, near or far, usually appears in focus (assuming you have good eyesight or appropriate glasses or contact lenses).

In landscape photography it is traditional to emulate this "everything-in-focus" view of the world by maximizing the depth of field. However, you can also choose to take a different approach. Whether it's creative intent or simply through necessity, you may be led to taking pictures with a much narrower depth of field.

> ### Tip
>
> *Remember that aperture numbers are really **fractions**, so f/16 is a small aperture, while f/4 is large. The D3100's Information Display (in **Graphic** mode) includes an illustration corresponding to the lens aperture.*

Three main factors determine depth of field: the focal length of the lens, the aperture, and the distance to the subject. As focal length and subject distance are often determined by other factors, aperture is key. The simple rule is: small aperture = big depth of field, and vice versa.

Long focal lengths produce less depth of field than wide-angles, so to increase the depth of field you would naturally think of fitting a wide-angle lens. However, this also changes other elements, making the situation slightly more complex. For example, suppose your main subject is a tree. To make sure that every branch and twig is sharp you will need good depth of field, so you might fit a wide-angle lens or zoom out to a wider focal length setting. However, you would then have to move in closer to keep the tree the same size in the frame, and moving closer to the subject *reduces* depth of field, losing at least some of the benefits of changing focal length. Moving closer also changes perspective and the apparent shape of the subject.

If you're photographing a broad landscape, rather than a single tree, you may already have decided on the viewpoint and angle you want, so changing the lens may not be an option, but in other instances it is well worth thinking about the impact that a change in focal length would have.

F/4

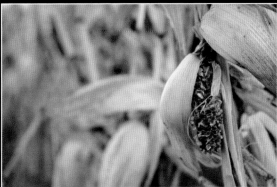

F/11

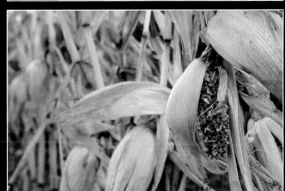

F/32

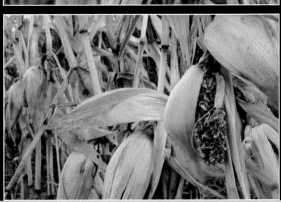

DEPTH OF FIELD »
The same setup, focused on the foreground corn, taken at f/4, f/11, and f/32, shows the effect on depth of field. Note the motion-blur due to the longer shutter-speed in the f/32 shot.

ISO: 400
Focal Length: 85mm
Shutter Speed: varies

Depth of field preview

When you look through the D3100's viewfinder, the lens is set at its widest aperture; if a smaller aperture is selected, it will stop down at the moment the picture is actually taken. This means that the image in the viewfinder may exhibit a smaller depth of field than the final photo.

Unlike Nikon's professional DSLRs, the D3100 does not have a depth of field preview button. This was essential on 35mm SLRs, as it would stop the lens down to the selected aperture, giving a sense of the depth of field in the final image.

However, there is an alternative that you can use with the D3100 whenever time allows. This involves taking a test shot and checking the image on the rear LCD, perhaps zooming in for a closer look. You could call it depth of field *review*. This can give a better sense of depth of field than the preview button ever did, but it is significantly slower. Still, many people would argue that it's good to slow down and take a little more time—even if it's just a few seconds—to think about what you are doing and what you hope to achieve.

Hyperfocal distance

When you really need an image to be sharp from front to back, remember that depth of field extends both in front of, and behind, the point of focus. If you focus at infinity, there's nothing beyond that, so you are in effect wasting some of your depth of field. In fact, depth of field extends two thirds behind the point of focus and one third in front of it, which is why you will frequently see or hear advice suggesting that you should "focus one third of the way into the picture." However, this doesn't make sense: it is mathematically impossible to define what is one third of the way from "here" to infinity.

What this advice is hinting at is that you should focus at the *hyperfocal distance*. This is the closest point at which you need to focus to make sure that the depth of field extends to infinity, and no further. It is, in effect, the maximum possible depth of field you can achieve.

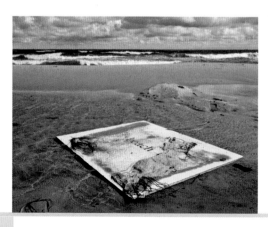

MAXIMIZING DEPTH OF FIELD   **«**
I wanted everything from the nearest ripple to the breaking waves to be sharp, and focusing at the hyperfocal distance helped make it so.

ISO: 320   *Focal Length:* 21mm
Shutter Speed: 1/400th sec.   *Aperture:* f/11

The hyperfocal distance (or hyperfocal point) is not a fixed distance—it varies depending on the focal length and aperture being used. There are tables and calculators that you can use to work out the hyperfocal distance, but there is also a rough-and-ready approach that will allow you to quickly establish the hyperfocal distance in the field.

Start by focusing on infinity—in practice, the most distant object in the scene, such as the horizon or skyline. Take a test shot at your chosen aperture setting and review the image on the rear LCD screen. Locate the *nearest* object that appears sharp: this is the hyperfocal point. You can now refocus on this object/at this distance to achieve the maximum depth of field with your chosen focal length and aperture combination.

> **Tip**
>
> *If you change the aperture setting or focal length of your lens, the hyperfocal distance changes also.*

Note:
It's highly likely that the D3100's Landscape mode uses the hyperfocal principle to keep both foreground and background in focus as far as possible. However, it does not always set the smallest possible aperture, so for fuller control use Aperture Priority (**A**).

Apparent sharpness

The previous definition of depth of field referred to objects *appearing to be sharp*. This is because details that look "soft" in a large print may appear sharp in a small print or a Web image, so depth of field is a relative value rather than an absolute. It's easy to forget this and become obsessive about always using the smallest apertures and determining the hyperfocal distance, but this may not always be necessary.

A full-screen review is often all that's needed to check sharpness and depth of field, and certainly one or two presses on the ⊕ button is sufficient for images that will be printed small or used on-screen.

For various reasons, images shot with the D3100, or any DX-format camera, will have greater depth of field than comparable images shot on a 35mm SLR or "full-frame" digital camera. This gain is only partly offset by the extra enlargement needed in printing.

Photographing motion

Motion is another area where the camera doesn't see what the eye sees. After all, we see movement, but the camera produces still images. However, movement can be very effectively conveyed in a still photograph, and it often reveals drama and grace that may be missed with the naked eye.

3

Freezing the action

Dynamic posture and straining muscles shout "movement," even in a figure frozen by a fast shutter speed. In fact the pin-sharp definition of muscles or facial expression can enhance the feeling of dynamism. But what is a "fast" shutter speed? Do you need to use the D3100's maximum 1/4000 sec. every time?

The second answer is definitely "no," but the first is harder to determine. The exact shutter speed needed to capture a sharp, frozen image depends on various factors: not just the speed of the subject, but its size and distance also. What really matters is the scale of movement in relation to the image frame. It can be easier to get a sharp image of a train traveling at 200mph than of a mountain biker doing 20mph, because you need to be so much closer to the latter. The direction of movement is another factor:

subjects traveling across the frame need faster shutter speeds than those moving toward the camera or away from it.

As a result, there is no "right" shutter speed, but you can play safe by setting the fastest shutter speed possible under the prevailing light conditions, as the D3100's Sports mode does.

For more control, Shutter Priority (**S**) is the obvious exposure mode to use, but check your images on the rear LCD screen

Tip

There's a simple "back-door" method to making certain you're always using the fastest possible shutter speed for the conditions: use Aperture Priority and select the widest available aperture. If the speed still doesn't seem fast enough, increase the ISO setting.

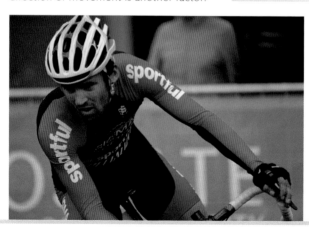

**SHUTTER SPEED TO «
FREEZE MOVEMENT**
A fast shutter speed freezes the action very effectively.

ISO: 640
Focal Length: 200mm
Shutter Speed: 1/1250 sec.
Aperture: f/4.5

whenever possible and, if a faster shutter speed appears necessary, be prepared to increase the ISO setting. If you shoot a particular activity on a regular basis, you'll soon discover what works for your particular needs.

Panning

With subjects moving across the field of view, panning is an excellent way to convey a sense of movement. By following the subject with the camera, it is recorded crisply while the background becomes blurred. The exact effect varies, so experimentation is advisable, preferably well before a critical shoot. Relatively slow shutter speeds are usually employed: anything from 1/8 sec.–1/125 sec. can work, and you may even go outside this

range. As Sports mode can't accommodate this, Shutter Priority (**S**) or Manual (**M**) are the logical alternatives.

Panning is usually easiest with a standard or short telephoto lens, but the decision may be out of your hands if the shooting distance is fixed (photographing from behind barriers at a sports event, for example). To help ensure a smooth panning movement during the exposure, keep following through as you press the shutter, and even after that.

SHUTTER SPEED FOR CREATIVE BLUR ⌄
An ideal situation for a panning shot: regular movement across the field of view. The figure isn't perfectly sharp, but still stands out well against the blurred surroundings.

ISO: 160 *Focal Length:* 29mm
Shutter Speed: 1/50 sec. *Aperture:* f/14

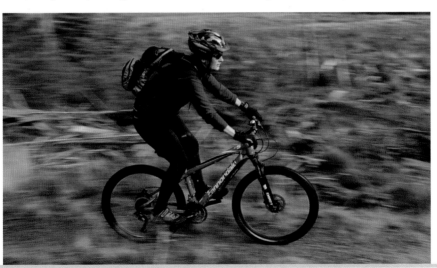

Blur

Another way to imply movement is with blur. This may be a necessity, because you just can't set a fast enough shutter speed, or it may be a creative choice, such as the silky effect achieved by photographing waterfalls with exposures lasting whole seconds rather than fractions. For other moving subjects, slightly faster speeds may well be more effective. To ensure that only the moving elements are blurred (for instance, the water blurs, but rocks remain sharp), secure the camera on a tripod or other solid support. Again, Sports mode is not appropriate and Shutter Priority (**S**) is the obvious choice.

You can also try for a more impressionistic effect by handholding the camera at a slow shutter speed. This doesn't work so well for waterfalls, but can sometimes be highly effective when shooting sports, dancers, and so on. It's always a bit hit-and-miss, but your success rate will definitely improve with practice.

Camera shake

Sometimes you'll move the camera intentionally for creative effect—panning is a common example—but unintentional movement is another story. Camera shake can produce anything from a slight loss of sharpness to a hopeless mess. Careful handling or the use of a camera support, such as a tripod or beanbag, will help to alleviate it, and Nikon also make several Vibration Reduction (VR) lenses.

Tip

To add something extra to your panned or blurred shots, consider using a discreet amount of flash. This gives a perfectly sharp image of the subject against a blurred background. The D3100's flash metering is very good at balancing exposures between the subject and background, but you may still want to experiment and change the settings (using flash compensation) to get results you like. There's no substitute for trial and error!

FLASH AND BLUR »

A discreet amount of fill-in flash sharpens up the figure while the background stays blurred.

ISO: 250 *Focal Length:* 22mm
Shutter Speed: 1/40 sec. *Aperture:* f/11

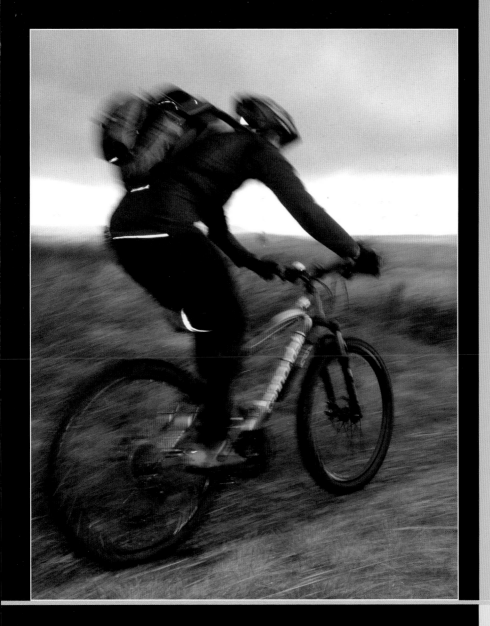

3 » COMPOSITION

Composition is an innocuous word for something that causes endless frustration and confusion. In its widest sense, it is the reason why some photos can be perfectly exposed and focused and yet have no emotional or aesthetic impact, while others may be technically flawed yet heart-stopping. Every time you take a picture you make decisions (consciously or unconsciously) about where to shoot from, where to aim the camera, how wide a view you want, what to include and what to leave out. These are essentially what composition is all about.

Personally, I try to avoid the C-word altogether; I prefer to talk about framing, which relates much better to what photographers actually do. Jettisoning the word "composition" also helps liberate us

from its associated baggage, particularly "rules of composition," such as the grossly overrated "Rule of Thirds." The real problem with this is that it is so often treated as not just a rule but as an unbreakable law. In fact, the best you can say of it is that it is a guideline or suggestion, and just one of many options you could try.

The great Ansel Adams said many wise things about photography, and none were wiser than this: "There are no rules for good photographs, there are only good photographs."

Rules are made to be broken, so it's principles that really help. There are two basic principles underpinning effective framing; *know where the edges are* and *see what the camera sees.*

Even if you want to use a "rule" of framing, you can't apply it without reference to the edges of the frame. The edges define the picture, and

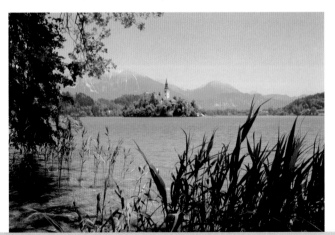

FRAMING «
Framing is about seeing a picture as a complete entity.

ISO: 200
Focal Length: 18mm
Shutter Speed: 1/100 sec.
Aperture: f/14

the picture is everything within them. Our eyes and brains are very good at selecting specific parts of a scene, but the camera doesn't make the same distinction. It will happily record the bits you are interested in and the bits you didn't even notice, frequently producing pictures that seem cluttered or confusing: hence the importance of seeing what the camera sees, not just what you *want* to see.

Looking through a traditional viewfinder, even a good one like the D3100's, is rather like looking through a window. Here it could be interesting to experiment with Live View mode. Now, instead of looking through a viewfinder, you're looking at a screen. If the viewfinder is like a window, the screen is like a picture

Note:
The D3100's viewfinder shows only 95% of the width and height of the full image, which can mean that distractions—unseen in the viewfinder—can appear around the edges of the final image. However, this is not unique to the D3100; it is true of most DSLRs from all manufacturers, with only the top-of-the-range professional cameras providing 100% viewfinder coverage. Of course, it's easy to crop the image to match the scene that you had in the viewfinder, but that's not exactly the point.

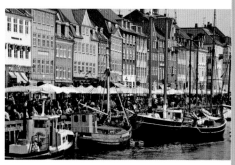

MULTIPLE ELEMENTS ⌃
There's no specific subject in this image. Every element plays its part.

ISO: 100 *Focal Length:* 95mm
Shutter Speed: 1/400 sec. *Aperture:* f/8

and, of course, it's a picture that we ultimately want.

I've yet to see any scientific studies, but intuition would suggest that using the screen to frame your shots might make it easier to see the whole picture—the bits you're interested in *and* the bits you aren't. However, using Live View all the time isn't recommended; it makes handling more awkward, drains batteries quickly, and can be unclear in bright sunlight. A viewfinder is far superior for most shooting, although the "Live View Picture" approach is still a worthwhile exercise.

When you go back to using the viewfinder, make a conscious effort to see it as a picture: look at the whole image, take note of the edges and what's included, and consciously seek out distracting and irrelevant elements.

Framing the landscape

Landscape photography poses special challenges in relation to framing, because—unlike portraits, for example—there's rarely a single subject. Landscape is boundless. The first challenge is simply choosing which segment of it you want to photograph. This means being selective and looking for the essence of a place in an attempt to try and catch what makes it appeal to you. Remember the old saying—"can't see the wood for the trees."

"Views" are fine, but landscapes are an all-round sensory experience. Many photographic "views" end up looking small, or flat, or otherwise disappointing, and often there's a very simple reason for this: there is no foreground.

Including the foreground does many things. It shows texture and detail, evoking sounds and smells and the rest of the sensory totality. The foreground can bring life and crispness where the distant scene is hazy or flatly-lit and, above all, including the foreground connects you to the place, distinguishing your shots from the detached views that anyone might get from a bus or train window.

Foregrounds can also help to convey depth and distance, and strengthen a sense of scale. If you want a photo of a mountain that conveys a sense of its awesome size, filling the picture with it may not be the best way. For many people, a shot of a peak in isolation is hard to "read," but including a relatively familiar object, such as a tree, helps us make sense of the unfamiliar. Human figures are also ideal for this, because we all know how small we are. Making the figure really tiny in the frame is often very effective, as long as it's still recognizably human.

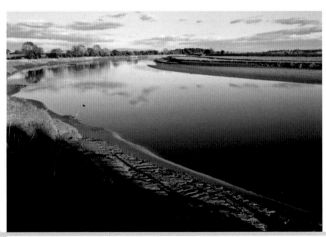

WIDE ANGLE «
PERSPECTIVE
A wide-angle lens was needed to encompass the broad sweep of this river near its estuary.

ISO: 160
Focal Length: 18mm
Shutter Speed: 1/40 sec.
Aperture: f/14

To get strong foregrounds in your pictures, the first principle is to get close. The second is to get closer. Use the third dimension: sit, kneel, crouch, crawl, or climb. Wide-angle lenses are brilliant for encompassing both the foreground and the distant vista. The D3100 has a 1.5x magnification factor, so a typical wide-angle zoom with a minimum focal length of 18mm gives the same coverage as a 27mm lens on a 35mm SLR or a full-frame

DSLR such as Nikon's D3s. As a result, photographers looking to make the most of the foreground, or big vistas, will hanker after an ultra-wide-angle lens, such as the 12–24mm f/4G ED-IF AF-S DX Nikkor.

Not every landscape is on the grand scale, and small details can also convey the essence of a place. If the light is not magical, and distant prospects look flat or hazy, then details, textures and the miniature landscapes of a rock-pool or forest clearing can bring your pictures back to life. Variations in scale, focus, and so on can also help liven up a sequence of pictures: an unrelieved display of expansive landscape images can eventually become oppressive.

POINTS OF INTEREST ⌄
There are several "points of interest" here—the young walkers, the farmhouse, and the distinctive outline of the Langdale Pikes. The image is about all of these, and more.

ISO: 200 *Focal Length:* 50mm
Shutter Speed: 1/160 sec. *Aperture:* f/9

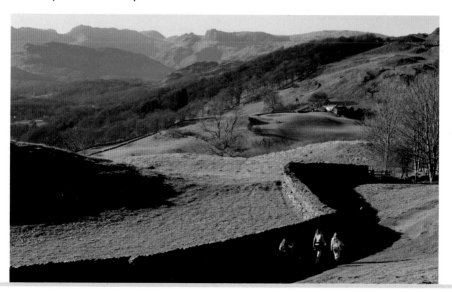

What makes a good photograph? For that matter, what makes any photograph? The answer is light. You can take photographs without a lens, or even without a camera, but not without light. Because it's universal, it's easy to take it for granted, to think "the camera will take care of it," and up to a point this is true: the D3100 is very good at dealing with varying amounts of light. However, there's much more to light than whether there's a lot or a little of it, and it really is worth tuning in to all the ways in which it varies: color, direction, and so on.

Light sources

Natural light essentially means sunlight, whether it's direct or indirect. Even moonlight is reflected sunlight. The sun itself varies little, but by the time it reaches the camera its light can be modified in many ways by the Earth's atmosphere and by reflection. As a direct light-source, the sun is very small, giving strongly directional light and hard-edged shadows, yet on an overcast day the same light can be spread across the entire sky, providing soft, even illumination. Studio photographers use massive "softboxes" to replicate this effect, but the closest the average user can get—at least on a small scale—is usually with bounce flash.

Beyond sun and flash there are many other artificial light sources, such as incandescent and fluorescent. Their color can vary enormously—making the D3100's white balance controls a blessing. However, their other qualities—such as direction and contrast—can usually be best understood by comparing them with more familiar sunlight and flash.

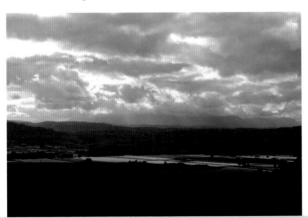

LIGHT-SHAFTS   **«**
A shaft of light transforms a "dull" day.

ISO: 320
Focal Length: 48mm
Shutter Speed: 1/400 sec.
Aperture: f/13

Contrast and dynamic range

Contrast, dynamic range, and tonal range are all terms used to refer to the range of brightness between the brightest and darkest areas of a scene or subject. Our eyes are very adaptable, and can generally see detail in both bright areas and deep shade, to a degree that even the best camera can't always match. In high-contrast conditions it's all too common that either the brightest highlights, such as white clouds or snow, end up completely blank and white, or that the deepest shadows turn dead black. "Clipping," as it's called, can even affect both ends of the tonal scale simultaneously. High-contrast conditions typically occur when the sun shines from a clear sky and the clearer the sky, the higher the contrast.

In overcast or "soft" lighting conditions, the contrast is much lower. This is rarely ideal for wide landscapes, but can be excellent for portraits and detail shots. For some subjects soft light is highly desirable: photographers who specialize in shooting wild flowers, for example, will often carry diffusers to create it.

The D3100 offers some useful options for dealing with high contrast, notably Active D-Lighting and D-Lighting. Shooting RAW also gives some chance of recovering highlight and/or shadow detail in post-processing, but all of these can only help within limits. Sometimes it's simply impossible to capture the entire

brightness range of a scene in a single exposure, and both the histogram display and the highlights display will help to identify problems. One option may be to reframe your shot to exclude large areas at the extremes of the brightness range: small patches of dead black or white will go unnoticed in most pictures, but large, featureless areas will be conspicuous.

Tip

Even if the highlights display shows clipping when you review your images, some highlight detail may be recoverable if you shoot RAW files. However, it may still be worth bracketing your exposures.

HIGH DYNAMIC RANGE ⏬
High dynamic range poses a challenge for any photographer, but another name for it might be "exciting light"—it's found in many of the shots we're most likely to want to take.

ISO: 125 *Focal Length:* 150mm
Shutter Speed: 1/250 sec. *Aperture:* f/8

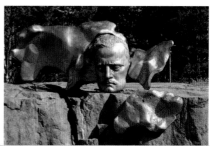

3

Digital imaging also offers another solution that was unavailable with film: HDR or High Dynamic Range imaging. This involves making multiple bracketed exposures—typically one for the bright areas, one that's right for the mid-tones and another for the shadows—that are later combined on the computer.

A solid tripod is essential to keep the images aligned, and it is also worth noting that this approach can become unusable if there's movement in the scene.

Tip

For close subjects, such as portraits, you can compensate for high contrast by adding some light to the shadows using the D3100's built-in flash or an accessory flash for fill-in light. Alternatively, you may prefer a reflector, which has the advantage that the effect is easily previewed. Dedicated photographic reflectors are available, but I often use a map, which I'm usually carrying anyway. Sometimes, natural reflectors are also available, such as light-colored rocks, white walls, or snow, for example, while a large white cloud can act as a "mega-reflector."

Direction of light

With direct sunlight or a single flashgun, the direction of the light source is obvious, but the same subject, seen from different angles, can appear totally different. At the other extreme, under an overcast sky, light comes from a broader area and so its quality varies much less with the viewing angle. Completely even lighting is quite rare and there's usually at least a vague sense of direction to it.

The effects of the direction of light are much easier to appreciate with a distinct main source such as direct sunlight. In simple terms, we refer to frontal lighting, oblique lighting, and backlighting.

Frontal lighting hits the subject head-on; it's what you get with on-camera flash, or with the sun behind you, flooding everything with light. While this might sound positive, the lack of shadows makes everything look flat and uniform. This can work well for subjects that derive their impact from pure color, shape, or pattern and, as true frontal lighting doesn't lead to extremes of contrast, the exposure is usually straightforward.

Oblique lighting (or side-lighting) is more complex than frontal lighting, and is therefore usually more interesting, creating shadows that emphasize form and texture, outlining hills and valleys. At really acute angles the light accentuates fine details,

LIGHTING OPTIONS ⌄

These three shots of the same subject, taken moments apart, show frontal, oblique, and backlighting respectively.

ISO: 400 ***Focal Length:*** 85mm
Other settings: various

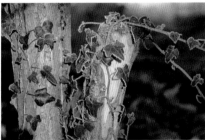

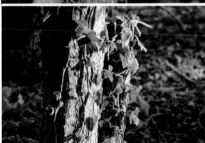

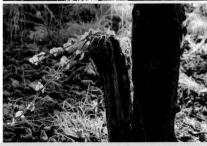

from crystals in rock to individual blades of grass. This is one reason why dedicated landscape photographers love the beginning and end of the day. However, in hillier terrain, even a high sun may still cast useful shadows. In some places, such as deep gorges, direct light only penetrates when the sun is high. What's key is not the height of the sun above the horizon, but the angle at which light strikes the subject. Oblique lighting is terrific for landscapes, and many other subjects, but is often accompanied by high contrast, making the exposure slightly harder to determine.

Backlighting can give striking and beautiful results in almost any sphere of photography—nature, portrait, or landscape—but it needs to be handled with care. By definition, a backlit subject will be in shadow and can easily appear as a mere silhouette. Sometimes this is exactly what you want: bare trees can look fantastic against a colorful sky. If so, meter for the bright areas to maximize color saturation, perhaps using exposure lock.

If you don't want a total silhouette, a reflector or fill-in flash can often help, but don't overdo it or you risk negating the backlit effect. Backlighting, combined with a reflector, is a simple way to get great portraits. Translucent materials such as foliage and fabric can glow beautifully when backlit, and they don't readily turn into silhouettes.

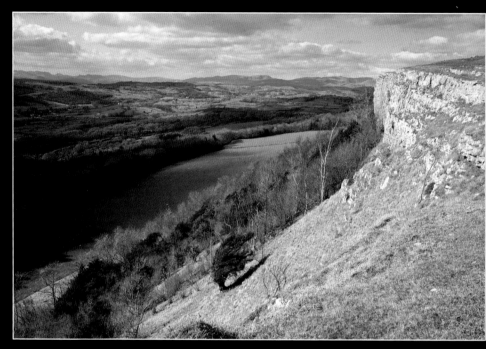

Settings

> *ISO:* 320
> *Focal Length:* 19mm
> *Shutter Speed:*
> 1/200 sec.
> *Aperture:* f/11

Frontal lighting can work well for landscapes and other subjects with strong shapes and colors: a few cloud shadows can help.

Oblique lighting gives a striking quality, but high contrast can be an issue.

Settings

> *ISO:* 200
> *Focal Length:* 80mm
> *Shutter Speed:*
> 1/400 sec.
> *Aperture:* f/5.6

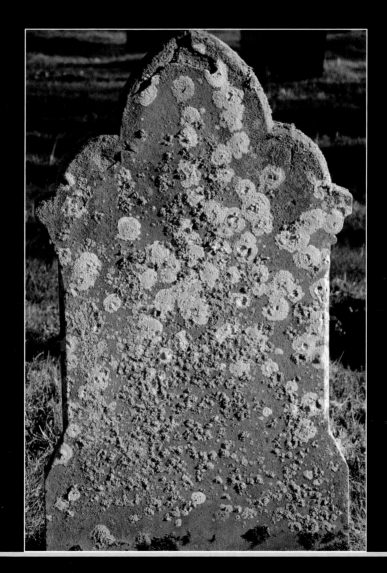

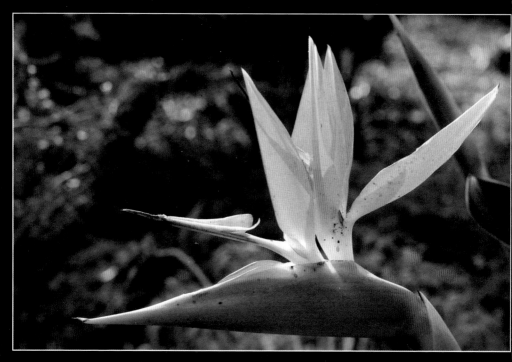

Settings

› *ISO:* 200
› *Focal Length:* 50mm
› *Shutter Speed:*
  1/400 sec.
› *Aperture:* f/5.6

Backlighting gives a unique luminosity ⌃
to the simplest of subjects.

» SOFT LIGHTING

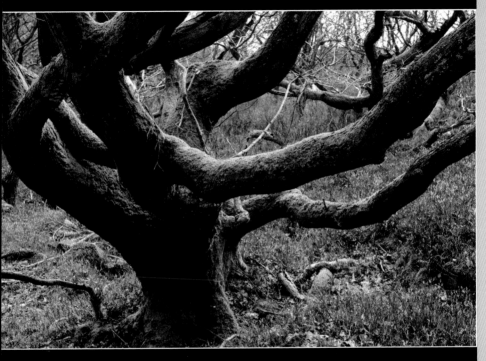

Settings
› *ISO:* 250
› *Focal Length:* 38mm
› *Shutter Speed:*
  1/15 sec.
› *Aperture:* f/13

Soft light works well where strong shapes ⌃
and/or colors are involved, and keeps
contrast within manageable limits.

3 » COLOR

A prism in a sunbeam reveals all of the colors of the rainbow, so the phrase "white light" is a misnomer at any time—natural light varies enormously in color.

Most of the time our eyes adjust automatically, so that we go on seeing green leaves as green, oranges as orange, and so on. Only at its most extreme, as in the intense red of the setting sun, are the changing colors of light really obvious.

It's all due to the way the sun's light is filtered by the atmosphere. When the sun is high in a clear sky the light is affected least, but when the sun is low, its path through the atmosphere is much longer and the light is shifted toward yellow and ultimately red, while the "lost," or scattered, light turns the sky blue.

The warmer light of a low sun is another reason why landscape photographers traditionally favor mornings and evenings. It's not just that we tend to find warm colors more pleasing; if that was all, the effect could be easily replicated with a Photoshop adjustment. In the real world, however, sunlit surfaces pick up a warm hue, while shadows receive light from the sky, tinting them blue. It's most obvious in snow scenes, but almost always true.

This difference in color between sunlit and shadow areas increases as the direct sunlight becomes redder, adding vibrancy to morning and evening shots. Filters can't duplicate this effect. When shifting colors are part of the attraction, you don't want to neutralize or "correct" them fully. However, if White Balance is set to **Auto** (as it is in Full Auto and Scene Modes), the D3100 will attempt to do exactly this. Try shooting in one of the user-control modes and changing the White Balance setting to **Direct sunlight** instead. Or shoot RAW, which allows you to adjust the color balance later.

Similar principles apply with artificial light. Sometimes you'll want to correct the color, but sometimes it's better left alone. Portraits shot under fluorescent lamps (even some "daylight" ones) can take on a ghastly greenish hue, which you will surely want to correct, and while Auto White Balance often improves matters, it isn't always perfect under artificial light.

On the other hand, if you're shooting floodlit buildings, the variations in color may be part of the appeal. The results you'll get with Auto White Balance are less predictable here and may not match either what you see or what you want. Night Landscape mode is an obvious choice, but, again, be prepared to take control of the white balance yourself.

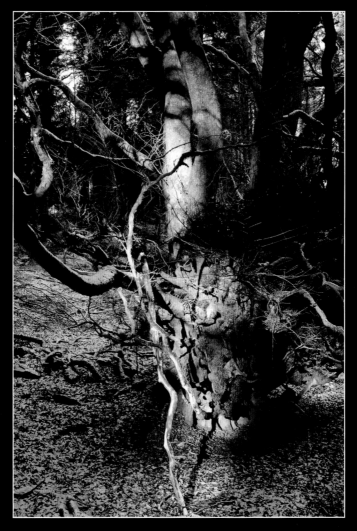

COLOR CONTRAST

The warm light of the winter sun contrasts in both intensity and color with cool shadows where light comes from the blue sky.

ISO: 800 ***Focal Length:*** 24mm ***Shutter Speed:*** 1/60 sec. ***Aperture:*** f/8

Flare

Lens flare results from stray light bouncing around within the lens. It's most prevalent when shooting toward the sun, whether the sun itself is in frame or just outside. It may produce a string of colored blobs, lined up as if radiating from the sun, or a more general veiling of light.

Advanced lens coatings, such as those used for Nikkor lenses, greatly reduce the incidence of flare, but keeping your lenses and filters scrupulously clean is still vital. Beyond that, if the sun's actually in the frame, some flare may be inescapable. It may diminish when the lens is stopped down, but if not, look for ways to reframe the shot or to mask the sun—behind a tree, for instance.

If the sun isn't actually in the frame, try to shield the lens from its direct rays. A good lens hood is essential, but further shading may be needed, especially with zoom lenses. You can provide this with a piece of card, a map, or even your hand. This is easiest with the camera on a tripod, otherwise it requires one-handed shooting (or a friend!). Check the viewfinder and/or monitor playback carefully to see if the flare has gone, and make sure the shading object hasn't crept into shot!

FLARE ⌄

Flare is evident in the first shot, but was eliminated easily by shading the lens.

ISO: 250 *Focal Length:* 24mm
Shutter Speed: 1/160 sec. *Aperture:* f/11

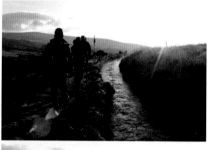

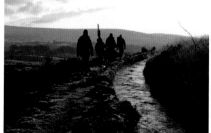

> #### *Tip*
>
> *Because the viewfinder does not show 100% of the image, the object you use to shade your lens with may appear at the edge of the picture. Check on playback for this. You can then adjust the object's position slightly or crop the image later.*

Distortion

Distortion makes things that are actually straight appear curved in the image. It's a result of lens design and as this continually improves it's less and less of an issue; the worst offenders are likely to be zoom lenses that are old, or cheap, or both, and distortion is often worst at the extremes of the zoom range.

When straight lines bow outward, it's called *barrel* distortion, and when they bend inward, it's *pincushion* distortion. Both problems can be prevented by activating Auto Distortion Control in Shooting menu; subsequently corrected using Distortion Control in the Retouch menu; or when you process your images with software such as *Nikon Capture NX2* or *Adobe Photoshop*. However, as all of these methods crop the image, it's better to avoid the issue in the first place by using good lenses.

Distortion may go unnoticed when shooting natural subjects with no straight lines, but can still rear its ugly head when a level horizon appears in a landscape or seascape, especially when that horizon is close to the top or bottom of the frame.

Chromatic Aberration

Chromatic aberration is a lens property that occurs when light rays from the subject aren't all focused together, so the light of different colors is focused in slightly different places on the sensor. This can be seen as colored fringing when images are examined closely. The D3100 has built-in correction for chromatic aberration during the processing of JPEG images, but with RAW images the only option is to correct it in post-processing.

Ideally, use lenses that minimize aberrations in the first place, although be aware that even slight chromatic aberration can be exaggerated by the way

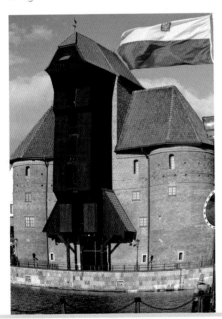

DISTORTION   «
Distortion was added in post-processing: if any lens gave this much distortion you'd either throw it away or call it a "semi-fisheye."

ISO: 320 *Focal Length:* 37mm
Shutter Speed: 1/320 sec. *Aperture:* f/13

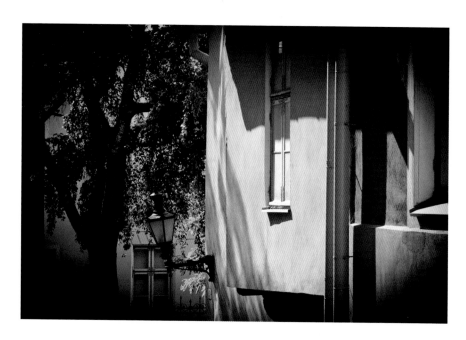

that the light strikes a digital sensor. If possible, it's best to use lenses that are designed specifically for digital cameras, such as Nikon's DX series.

Vignetting

Vignetting is a darkening toward the corners of the image, which is most conspicuous in even-toned areas such as clear skies. Almost all lenses have a slight tendency to vignette at maximum aperture, but it usually disappears on

VIGNETTE

A vignette effect was added in post-processing: some people feel that it can give an image a "period" atmosphere.

ISO: 400 *Focal Length:* 95mm
Shutter Speed: 1/320 sec. *Aperture:* f/11

stopping down. It can also be caused—or exaggerated—by using an unsuitable lens hood, filter holders, or by "stacking" multiple filters on the lens (rarely a good idea). Like most faults, it can be tackled in post-processing, but prevention is better than cure.

» DIGITAL ISSUES

Noise

Image noise is created by random variations in the amount of light recorded by each pixel, and appears as speckles of varying brightness or color. It is most obvious in areas that should have an even tone, especially in the darker areas of the image. Unfortunately, noise becomes more prevalent as the individual photosites on the sensor get smaller, which results from cramming more pixels onto the same size sensor. However, this has driven major improvements in the software that compensates for image noise. Although the D3100 has more than 14 million photosites on its 23.6 x 15.8mm sensor, its noise reduction abilities are excellent. This is often applied to JPEG images as part of in-camera processing, but you may prefer to apply noise reduction to RAW files during post-processing.

To minimize noise, shoot at the lowest ISO rating possible and expose carefully: underexposure increases the risk of visible noise. A tripod can be a big help.

NOISE ⌄

Noise is certainly evident, but flash would only have weakened the effect of the lights.

ISO: 6400 *Focal Length:* 13mm
Shutter Speed: 1/100 sec. *Aperture:* f/5.6

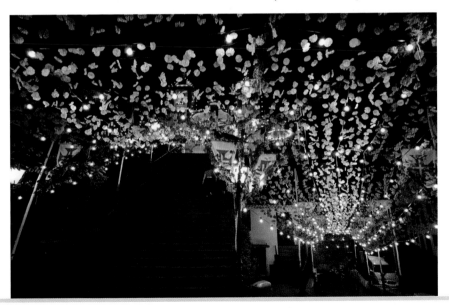

3

Clipping

Clipping occurs when either the highlights or shadows are recorded without detail, so shadows are pure black and/or highlights are pure white. Clipping can be detected as a "spike" at either extreme of the histogram display, and in full-frame playback you can also opt to have the D3100 show highlight clipping.

The D3100 is less prone to clipping than previous generations of cameras, but no camera is totally immune. There is some scope to recover clipped areas if you shoot RAW, while Active D-Lighting (and D-Lighting) can help with JPEGs.

Artifacts and Aliasing

When viewing a digital image we don't usually notice that it is made up of individual pixels, but small clumps of pixels can sometimes become apparent as "artifacts" of various kinds. They are usually more evident in low-resolution images,

BURNED-OUT HIGHLIGHTS ⌄

At first glance, the exposure appears fine, but a second look reveals areas in the white clouds where all detail has been clipped or burned out.

ISO: 160 ***Focal Length:*** 20mm
Shutter Speed: 1/160 sec. ***Aperture:*** f/13

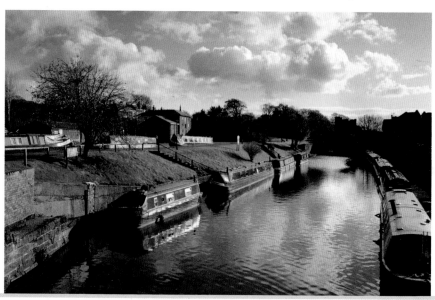

simply because of the smaller number (coarser "mapping") of pixels.

Aliasing is most evident on diagonal or curved lines, giving them a jagged or stepped appearance. *Moiré* or *maze artifacts* can occur when there's interference between areas of fine pattern in the subject and the grid pattern of the sensor itself. This often takes the form of aurora-like swirls or fringes of color. To compensate for such issues, digital cameras employ a low-pass filter directly in front of the sensor. This works by blurring the image slightly, which is very effective at removing artifacts, but means that images need to be resharpened either in-camera or during post-processing.

A further form of artifact is the *JPEG artifact*, which looks a lot like aliasing, but is created when JPEG images are

Tip

Repeatedly opening and re-saving JPEG images on a computer can multiply the effect of JPEG artifacts. If repeated edits are anticipated it is advisable to save the image as a TIFF first, and perform all editing operations on this version.

compressed heavily, either in-camera or on the computer. Avoid it by limiting JPEG compression and using the **Fine** setting for images that may later be printed or viewed at large sizes.

Sharpening images

Because of the low-pass filter, some sharpening is always required to make a digital camera's images look acceptable. However, too much sharpening can introduce artifacts, including white fringes or halos along defined edges.

JPEG images are sharpened during in-camera processing, with the sharpening settings accessed through the Set Picture Control option in the Shooting menu. Any changes to the sharpening level only affect images taken using that particular Picture Control, but it's always wise to be conservative about in-camera sharpening levels: you can add more later, but it's virtually impossible to take it away again.

With RAW images, sharpening takes place on the computer, either during the initial RAW conversion, or later. Sharpening at the RAW conversion stage is reversible, because the original file is saved untouched, so you can experiment with different levels of sharpening without permanent consequences.

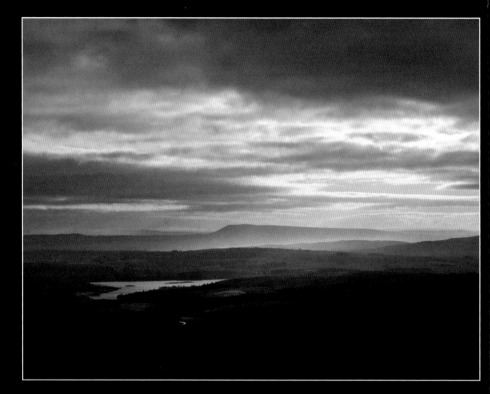

Settings

> *ISO:* 250
> *Focal Length:* 48mm
> *Shutter Speed:* 1/1000 sec.
> *Aperture:* f/9

Some people might have seen this as a dull day, ☆ but to me it was visually far more exciting than the average bright, sunny afternoon. Because the foreground was dark and relatively featureless moorland, I placed the horizon low in the frame. The broken clouds are a very important part of the picture.

» AGAINST THE LIGHT

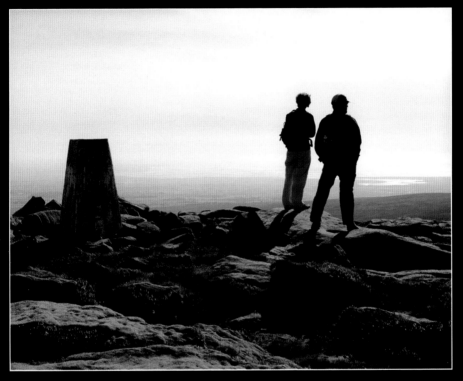

"Against the light" sounds strangely negative, as if ⌄
light is somehow the enemy, but a high proportion
of my favorite shots are taken "contre-jour." The
phrase "into the light" sounds much better. I'll often
turn away from a scene and then walk back toward
it, into the light. Unless time is very pressing, I'll
never leave the exposure entirely to the camera in
these situations; I'll always check the histogram and
then either use exposure compensation (in Aperture
Priority mode) or use Manual from the start.

Settings
> *ISO:* 320
> *Focal Length:* 41mm
> *Shutter Speed:*
  1/400 sec.
> *Aperture:* f/11

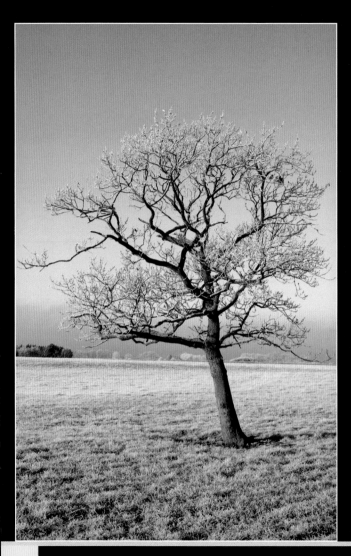

Less is more, they say, and **«**
it's often true in photography.
This was a wonderful morning,
very cold, but still and bright.
Every tree was covered in hoar
frost but this one appealed to
me because it stood alone. I
had to get reasonably close to
make sure none of the other
nearby trees would creep into
the frame, and I crouched
slightly to "lift" the tree above
the horizon so it would better
stand out.

Settings

> *ISO:* 160
> *Focal Length:* 35mm
> *Shutter Speed:*
  1/160 sec.
> *Aperture:* f/11

» ACTION IN THE LANDSCAPE

This shot sums up the challenge and rewards of a mountain bike trip along the West Highland Way. Having cycled up to a pass, this fabulous trail appeared before us. The lines of the trail leading toward the distant peaks immediately suggested this image—it felt as if the shot framed itself. I then got my companion (my nephew) to ride down the trail. As he's relatively small in the frame and moving fairly slowly at this point, a modest shutter speed was adequate to freeze the motion.

Settings
> *ISO:* 400
> *Focal Length:* 24mm
> *Shutter Speed:* 1/125 sec.
> *Aperture:* f/11

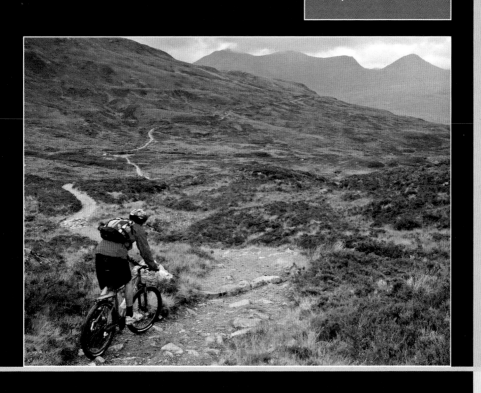

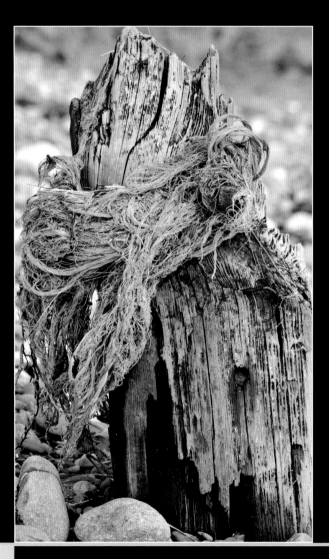

On a generally overcast «
walk from Barrow to Ulverston,
the wide open spaces of
Morecambe Bay played second
fiddle to intriguing details close
at hand. Strong light could well
have made this subject appear
confused and cluttered, but in
the soft light it was clear and
simple. I framed as tightly as I
could and used a fairly wide
aperture to soften the
background.

Settings
› *ISO:* 200
› *Focal Length:* 86mm
› *Shutter Speed:*
  1/400 sec.
› *Aperture:* f/7.1

» LONG-LENS LANDSCAPE

A very different take on ⌄
Morecambe Bay: the curves of the
channels hold the picture together
and the contrasting colors of
sunlight and cloud give it vibrancy.
The contrast was extremely high,
so shooting in RAW and processing
the image carefully was the only
way of achieving a result that
compared with the scene I had
actually witnessed.

Settings
> *ISO:* 100
> *Focal Length:* 200mm
> *Shutter Speed:*
  1/30 sec. (tripod)
> *Aperture:* f/16

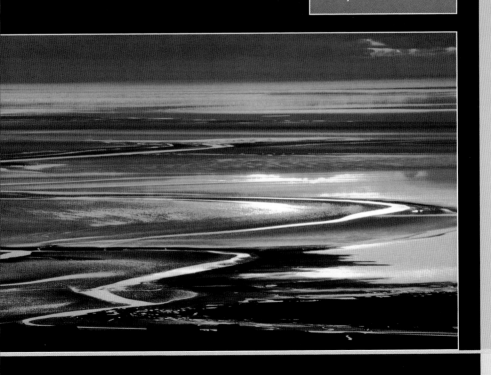

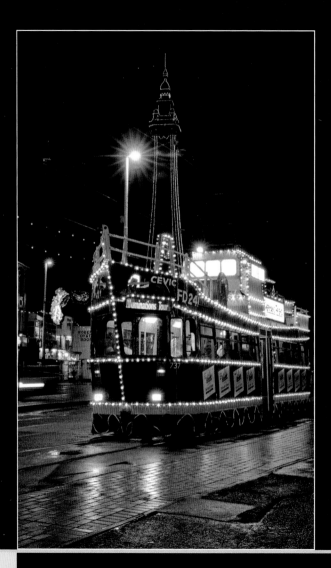

I wanted to shoot this illuminated tram with the iconic Blackpool Tower behind, but knew that the long exposure would blur a moving subject. I positioned myself close to a tram-stop and took the shot as soon as passengers had embarked and the doors had closed. I knew I wouldn't get another chance for around an hour, so I took several test shots before the crucial one.

Settings
> *ISO:* 400
> *Focal Length:* 37mm
> *Shutter Speed:*
  1 second (with tripod)
> *Aperture:* f/11

» OUTDOOR FLASH

What I'd hoped would be a fine sunrise was
mostly lost to unexpected cloud, but walking
through this band of woodland I saw the potential
for a very different image. Shooting in Manual
mode, I set an exposure that captured detail in the
background, then lit the foreground with a Nikon
Speedlight, positioned off-camera to the left and
fired by a remote cord.

Settings
> *ISO:* 800
> *Focal Length:* 24mm
> *Shutter Speed:*
> 1/10 sec. (with tripod)
> *Aperture:* f/14

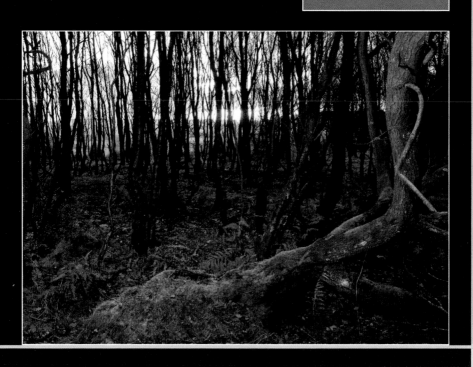

Chapter 4
FLASH

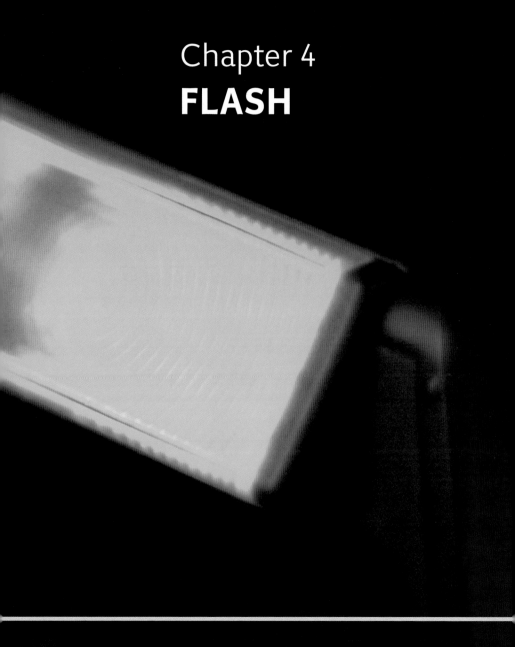

4 FLASH

The D3100 has great flash capabilities, whether using its own built-in flash or more powerful accessory units, but flash photography causes frequent confusion and frustration.

The full benefits are only seen if basic principles are grasped. What's fundamental is that all flashguns are small light sources and they are all relatively weak. This is especially true for built-in units such as the D3100's and most other DSLRs (those on compact cameras are typically even smaller and weaker). The small size of a flashgun gives its light a hard, one-dimensional quality. It's somewhat similar to direct sunlight, but even the strongest sunlight is slightly softened by scattering and reflection. However, there are various ways to soften and redirect the light.

The weakness of flash is an even more fundamental property. Essentially, all flashes have a limited range, and if the subject is too far away the flash simply can't deliver enough light. While the small size and limited power are common to all flash units, a third issue arises with built-in flash, namely its fixed position almost in line with the lens. The upshot is that flash—especially built-in flash—is not the answer to every low-light shot and understanding its limitations can help you understand when not to use flash, as well as when and how you can use it most effectively.

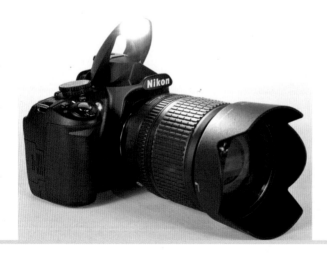

D3100 FLASH RAISED «

» GUIDE NUMBERS

In the past, determining flash exposures and the working range required calculations based on the Guide Number (**GN**) of each unit, which relates subject distance to the f-stop (aperture setting) in use. Guide numbers are specified in feet and/or meters and are usually given for an ISO rating of 100. However, there's no longer any requirement to memorize the formula that determines the working aperture for the flash at any given distance, as the D3100 has a very advanced flash metering system that will usually guarantee correct illumination.

The GN does, however, help us compare the power and range of different flashguns. It indicates, for example, that Nikon's SB-900 Speedlight is at least three times as powerful as the built-in unit, allowing it to expose a subject that's three times as far away, or let the photographer set a lower ISO and/or a smaller aperture. When comparing different units, be sure that the GNs given are using the same parameters: Nikon gives the GN for the D3100's built-in flash as 12 (meters) or 39 (feet) at ISO 100, for example.

FLASH RANGE »
The limited range of the built-in flash is apparent here, reaching only a short way into the tunnel. There is also a very obvious shadow of the lens hood on the ground.

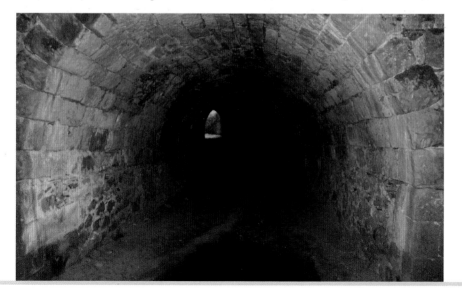

» FILL-IN FLASH

A key application for flash is as a "fill-in" light to lift dark shadows such as those cast by direct sunlight. This is why pros regularly use flash in bright sunlight (exactly when most people wouldn't think to use it). Fill-in flash doesn't need to illuminate the shadows fully, only lighten them a little, which means the flash can be used at a

FLASH FOR DETAIL

Fill-in flash: The background exposure is the same for both shots, but without flash the closest tree is a virtual silhouette.

ISO: 320 *Focal Length:* 16mm
Shutter Speed: 1/100 sec. *Aperture:* f/11

smaller aperture, or greater distance, than when it is the main lightsource.

i-TTL balanced fill-flash

As part of its Creative Lighting System (CLS), Nikon has developed i-TTL balanced fill-flash to help achieve natural-looking results when using fill-in flash. i-TTL balanced fill-flash automatically comes into play provided that matrix or center-weighted metering is selected and a CPU lens is attached, or lens data has been specified: most of the time, in other words. The flash

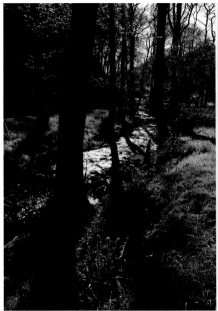

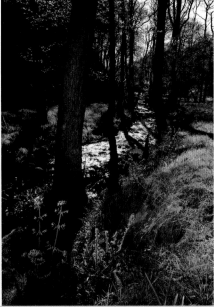

(either built-in or a compatible external unit) emits a series of virtually invisible pre-flashes immediately before exposure. Light reflected from these is detected by the metering sensor and analyzed together with the ambient light. If Type D or Type G lenses are used, distance information is also analyzed.

Standard i-TTL flash

If spot metering is selected, the Standard i-TTL flash mode is activated instead (it can also be selected directly on some accessory flashguns). Flash output is controlled to provide correct illumination of the subject, but background illumination is not taken into consideration. This mode is more appropriate when flash is being used as the main light source rather than for filling in shadows.

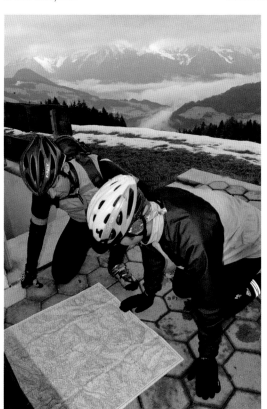

BALANCED FILL   **«**
i-TTL balanced fill-flash gives a very natural result; it's not glaringly obvious that flash has been used at all, but without it the foreground would be much darker.

ISO: 400
Focal Length: 18mm
Shutter Speed: 1/125 sec.
Aperture: f/10

» OPERATING THE BUILT-IN FLASH

The D3100's built-in flash, like all such units, is small, low-powered, and fixed in a position close to the lens axis. Low power limits working range, while its size and position produce a rather harsh frontal light which is—to say the least—unflattering for portraits (although occasionally better than nothing). The built-in flash really blossoms when used for fill-in light, and can also be used to trigger remote flashguns. The following assumes you are using **P**, **A**, **S**, or **M** modes: in Full Auto and Scene Modes the flash activates either automatically or not at all.

To use the built-in flash

1) Select a metering method: matrix or center-weighted metering is appropriate for fill-in flash using i-TTL balanced fill-flash. Spot metering is appropriate when flash is the main light.

2) Press ⚡ and the flash will pop up and begin charging. When it is charged, the ready indicator ⚡ is displayed in the viewfinder.

3) Choose a flash mode from the Active Information Display by highlighting the current mode and pressing (OK). Select the desired mode and press (OK) again.

4) Half-press the shutter-release button to focus and take a meter reading. Fully

depress the shutter-release button to take the photo.

5) When finished, lower the built-in flash by pressing down until it clicks into place.

› Auto flash

In AUTO Auto, 👤 Portrait, 👶 Child, 👤 Night portrait, and 🌷 Close up modes, the default setting is **Auto flash**, which means that the flash will operate automatically if the camera judges that the light levels are too low. Alternative modes that can be set are **Red-eye reduction** and

Flash off.
In 🚫 Auto (flash off), 🏔 Landscape, and 🏃 Sports modes, the effective mode is **Flash off** and this cannot be overridden (even if you fit a separate flash, the choices are limited to turning red-eye reduction on or off).

> **Tip**
>
> *The built-in flash is recommended for use with CPU lenses between 18mm and 300mm focal length. Some lenses may block part of the flash output at close range; removing the lens hood often helps. The D3100's manual details other limitations with certain lenses.*

In **P**, **A**, **S**, and **M** modes, Auto flash is not available—you must activate the flash by pressing ⚡.

Flash exposure

The combinations of shutter speed and aperture that are available when using flash depend on the exposure mode in use:

Exposure mode	Shutter Speed	Aperture
Auto / **Portrait** / **Child** / **P**	Set automatically by the camera. The normal range is between 1/200 sec. and 1/60 sec., but in certain modes all settings between 1/200 sec. and 30 sec. are available.	Set automatically by the camera.
S	Selected by user. All settings between 1/200 sec. and 30 sec. are available. If the user sets a fast shutter speed, the D3100 will fire at 1/200 sec. while the flash is active.	Set automatically by the camera.
A	Set automatically by the camera. The normal range is between 1/200 sec. and 1/60 sec., but in certain modes all settings between 1/250 sec. and 30 sec. are available.	Selected by user.
M	Selected by user. All settings from 1/200 sec.–30 sec. (and Bulb) are available. If the user sets a fast shutter speed, the D3100 will fire at 1/200 sec. when the flash is active.	Selected by user.
Close up	Set automatically by the camera. The normal range is between 1/200 sec. and 1/125 sec.	Set automatically by the camera. Maximum aperture limited to f/5.6 at ISO 200, f/8 at ISO 800, f/11 at ISO 3200.
Night portrait	Set automatically by the camera. The normal range is between 1/200 sec. and 1 sec.	Set automatically by the camera.

» FLASH RANGE

The range of any flash depends on its power, ISO sensitivity setting, and the aperture selected. The following table shows the approximate range of the built-in flash for selected distances, apertures, and ISO settings. These figures are based on the range table published in the D3100 manual and supported by practical tests.

It's not necessary to memorize all these figures, but it is helpful to have a general sense of the limited range that always applies when using flash. A few test shots will soon establish a working range that achieves good results for a given situation.

Tip

If the flash appears too weak, or the range is insufficient, turning up the ISO setting may help, but check first that flash compensation has not been activated.

	ISO equivalent setting					Range	
	100	200	400	800	1600	meters	feet
Aperture	1.4	2	2.8	4	5.6	1.0–8.5	3'3"–27'11"
	2	2.8	4	5.6	8	0.7–6.1	2'4"–20'
	2.8	4	5.6	8	11	0.6–4.2	2'–13'9"
	4	5.6	8	11	16	0.6–3.0	2'–9'10"
	5.6	8	11	16	22	0.6–2.1	2'–6'11"
	8	11	16	22	32	0.6–1.5	2'–4'11"
	11	16	22	32		0.6–1.1	2'–3'7"
	16	22	32			0.6–0.8	2'–2'7"

» FLASH SYNCHRONIZATION AND MODES

Flash, as the name implies, is virtually instantaneous. A burst of flash lasts just a few milliseconds, but if the flash is to cover the whole image frame it must be fired when the shutter is fully open. At faster shutter speeds, DSLRs such as the D3100 do not expose the whole frame at once. In the case of the D3100, the fastest shutter speed that can be used with flash is 1/200 sec. This is therefore known as the sync (*synchronization*) speed.

The D3100 has several flash modes, and the differences between them are largely to do with synchronization and shutter speed. Choose a flash mode by pressing ⚡ and rotating the command dial. In **P**, **A**, **S**, or **M** modes you will need to press the

button once to raise the flash, then press it again to choose the flash mode. The flash mode can also be selected through the Active Information Display—the flash item appears bottom left—or the Guide Menu (under Advanced operation).

Standard flash mode (front curtain sync)

This is the default flash mode when using the **P**, **A**, **S**, or **M** exposure modes, and is ideal when you need to respond quickly. In standard mode, the flash fires as soon as the shutter is fully open, so as quickly as possible after the shutter-release button is pressed. In **P** and **A** exposure modes, the camera will set a shutter speed in the range 1/60–1/200 sec.

> **Note:**
> For some reason Nikon has changed its terminology and now labels the basic flash mode as "Fill-flash" on the D3100. This is accurate when using matrix or centerweighted metering, but not when spot metering is active.

SLOW SYNC FLASH «
Slow sync flash allows the background to register in low-light shots.

ISO: 1600 *Focal Length:* 16mm
Shutter Speed: 1/30 sec. *Aperture:* f/4.5

Slow sync

This mode allows longer shutter speeds (up to 30 seconds) to be used in **P** and **A** exposure modes, so that the background can be recorded, even in low ambient light. Movement of the subject or camera (or even both) can result in a partly blurred image combined with a sharp image where the subject is lit by the flash. This may be unwanted, but can also be used intentionally for creative effect.

This mode is also available, in a more limited form, with  **Night portrait** mode, when the longest exposure is limited to 1 second. Slow sync cannot be selected when shooting in **S** and **M** exposure modes, but isn't necessary as longer shutter speeds are available.

Rear curtain sync

Rear curtain sync triggers the flash not at the first available moment (as per front curtain sync), but at the last possible instant, just before the second shutter curtain starts to close. This makes sense when photographing moving subjects because any image of the subject created by the ambient light then appears *behind* the sharp flash image, which looks more natural than having it appear to extend ahead of the direction of movement. Rear curtain sync can only be selected when using **P**, **A**, **S**, and **M** exposure modes. In **P** and **A** modes it also allows slower shutter speeds (below 1/60 sec.) to be used, and is then called **slow rear curtain sync**. Shooting with rear curtain sync can be

SLOW SYNC «

Slow sync combines a flash image with a motion-blurred image from the ambient light, but front-curtain sync makes the latter trail ahead of the flash image, not behind it.

ISO: 160
Focal Length: 36mm
Shutter Speed: 1/15 sec.
Aperture: f/16

tricky at longer exposure times, as you need to predict where your subject will be at the *end* of the exposure, rather than immediately after pressing the shutter-release button. It is often best suited to working with cooperative subjects so that the timing can be fine-tuned after reviewing the images on the LCD screen.

Red-eye reduction

On-camera flash, especially the built-in unit, is very prone to "red-eye," where light reflects off the subject's retina. In animals you may see colors other than red (green is common).

Red-eye reduction works by shining a light (the AF-assist illuminator) at the subject just before the exposure, causing the subject's pupils to contract. This delay makes it inappropriate with moving subjects, and kills spontaneity. Most of the time, it's far better to remove red-eye using the Red-eye correction facility in the Retouch menu or on the computer. Better still, use a separate flash, away from the lens axis, or no flash at all, perhaps shooting at a higher ISO rating.

Red-eye reduction with slow sync

Self-evidently, this combines the two modes named, allowing backgrounds to register, while countering the chance of red-eye. This mode is only available when using **P** and **A** exposure modes and, in a more limited form, **Night portrait**.

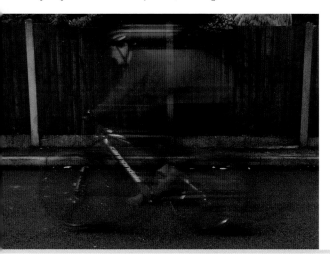

REAR CURTAIN **«**
Rear curtain sync means that the motion-blurred part of the image trails behind the sharp image created by the flash.

ISO: 160
Focal Length: 36mm
Shutter Speed: 1/15 sec.
Aperture: f/16

Although the D3100's flash metering is extremely sophisticated, you may still want to adjust the flash output, perhaps for creative effect. Playing back images on the monitor makes it easy to assess the effect of the flash, allowing flash compensation to be applied with confidence for subsequent shots.

To use flash compensation, call up the Active Information Display. The flash compensation item is midway along the bottom of the screen. Compensation can be set from -3EV to +1EV in increments of ⅓EV. Positive compensation will brighten

areas lit by the flash, while leaving other areas of the image unaffected. Be aware, though, that if the flash is already at the limit of its range, positive compensation can't make it any brighter.

Negative compensation reduces the brightness of flash-lit areas, again leaving other areas unaffected. After use, be sure to reset the flash compensation to zero, otherwise the camera will retain the setting and apply it the next time flash is used.

Note:
Flash compensation works similarly when a compatible Speedlight such as the SB-900 or SB-700 is attached.

Tip

Flash compensation can also be set by pressing ⚡ *and* ±🔲 *and rotating the command dial. Some users find this easier than using the Active Information Display.*

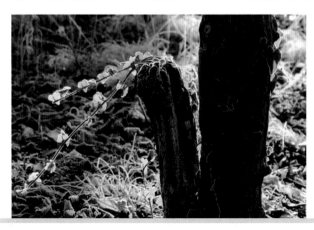

FLASH EXPOSURE »
COMPENSATION
The three shots (*opposite*) were taken with flash compensation set to +1EV, 0, and −1EV respectively. The background exposure remains the same. Some may prefer the result with no flash at all (*left*).

ISO: 400
Focal Length: 52mm
Shutter Speed: 1/60 sec.
Aperture: f/11

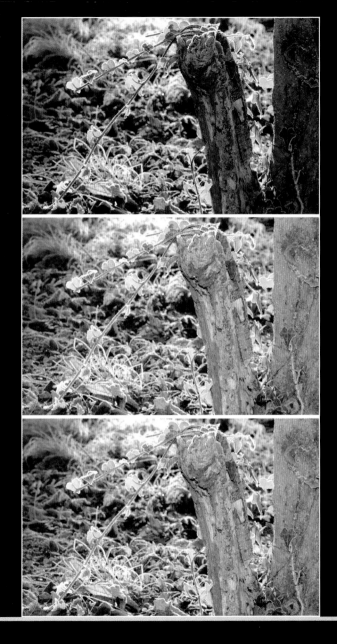

If you're serious about portrait or close-up photography in particular, you'll soon find the built-in flash inadequate. Accessory flashes, which Nikon calls Speedlights, extend the power and flexibility of flash with the D3100 enormously.

For outstanding results using flash, Nikon's Creative Lighting System is hard to beat, and to take full advantage of it really requires a Nikon Speedlight. The current range offers six models, all highly sophisticated units aimed primarily at professional and advanced users, and priced accordingly. The flagship SB-900 is particularly impressive—but then it ought to be: its price is not far short of a D3100!

Independent makers such as Sigma offer alternatives, many of which are also compatible with Nikon's i-TTL flash control, although these "dedicated" units are still not exactly cheap.

However, a great range of possibilities can be explored with much cheaper units. For instance, any flash unit, however basic, that has a "test" button allowing it to be fired manually can be used for the "painting with light" technique outlined opposite. You may have an old flash at the back of a cupboard somewhere, and it's also worth looking in the bargain bin at the local camera store. There is only space in this book to cover Nikon's own units.

Mounting an external Speedlight

1) Check that the camera and the Speedlight are both switched **OFF**, and that the built-in flash is down. Remove the hotshoe cover.

2) Slide the foot of the Speedlight into the camera's hotshoe. If it does not slide easily, check whether the mounting lock on the Speedlight is locked.

3) Rotate the lock lever at the base of the Speedlight to secure it in position.

4) Switch on both the camera and flash.

> ### Tip
>
> *A flash uses a lot of battery power, so if you are using a Speedlight it is a good idea to carry at least one set of spare cells.*

» BOUNCE AND OFF-CAMERA FLASH

The fixed position of the D3100's built-in flash can throw shadows on close subjects and give portraits a "police mugshot" look. A separate Speedlight mounted in the hotshoe improves things slightly, but you can make a much bigger difference by either bouncing the flash off a ceiling, wall, or reflector, or taking the Speedlight off the camera.

Bounce flash

Bouncing the flash off a suitable surface both spreads the light (softening hard-edged shadows), and changes its direction, producing better modeling on the subject.

Nikon's SB-900, SB-800, SB-700, and SB-600 Speedlights all have heads that can be tilted and swiveled through a wide range of angles, allowing the light to be bounced off walls, ceilings, and other surfaces. The SB-400 has a more limited tilt capability, but this still enables the light to be bounced off the ceiling or a reflector.

FLASH DIRECTION »

The first shot (*right*) was taken using the built-in flash. Despite some ugly shadows, this very three-dimensional subject looks distinctly flat.

The second image uses indirect flash from the left, which provides more interesting light and adds depth.

The third image uses bounced flash to give a much softer, more even light, but it retains most of the subject's three-dimensional quality.

ISO: 3200
Focal Length: 105mm
Shutter Speed: 1/125 sec.
Aperture: f/11

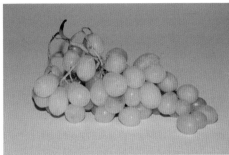

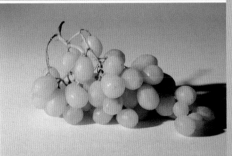

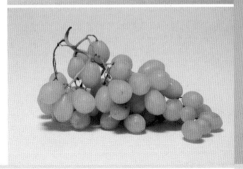

Off-camera flash

Taking the flash off the camera gives you complete control over the direction of its light, and Nikon's dedicated remote cords will also preserve i-TTL metering.

Painting with light

This intriguing technique can be employed with any flashgun, even the cheapest, provided it can be triggered manually. You could even use the built-in flash of a second camera! By firing repeated flashes at a static subject from various directions, you can build up the coverage of light without losing the sparkle that directional light gives. Some trial and error will be needed, but that's part of the fun.

1) Set up so that neither the camera nor the subject will move during the exposure.

2) Use Manual (**M**) mode (nothing else will do) and set a long shutter speed of 20–30 seconds, or even switch to **B**. Set a small aperture such as f/16 (this may need trial and error) and focus on the subject. Set the focus to manual so the camera doesn't try to refocus.

3) Turn out the lights. It helps to have just enough background light to see what you are doing, but no more.

4) Trigger the shutter and fire the flash at the subject from different directions. Don't aim it directly into the lens.

5) After the exposure, review the result and start again! For example, if the result is too bright, use fewer flashes, a lower ISO, a smaller aperture, fire from further away, or a combination of these. If the flash has a variable power setting this could be turned down also.

» NIKON SPEEDLIGHTS

	SB-900	SB-800	SB-700	SB-600	SB-400
Guide Number for ISO 100 (meters/feet)	34/111.5	38/125	28/92	30/98	21/69
Angle of coverage (widest focal length covered) with D3100	12mm	16mm	16mm	16mm	18mm
Tilt/swivel	Yes	Yes	Yes	Yes	Tilt only
Dimensions (width x height x depth)	3.07 x 5.75 x 4.67in (78 x 146 x 118.5mm)	2.78 x 5.10 x 3.66in (70.5 x 129.5 x 93mm)	2.80 x 4.96 x 4.11in (71 x 126 x 104.5mm)	2.68 x 4.86 x 3.54in (68 x 123.5 x 90mm)	2.60 x 2.22 x 3.15in (66 x 56.5 x 80mm)
Weight (without batteries)	14.64oz (415g)	12.35oz (350g)	12.70oz (360g)	10.58oz (300g)	4.48oz (127g)
Use as Commander?	Yes	Yes	No	No	No

The table above summarizes the key features of Nikon's current Speedlight models:

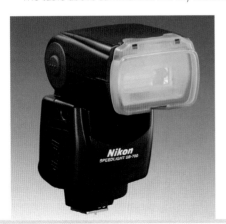

Wireless Flash

Nikon's Creative Lighting System includes the ability to control multiple Speedlights through a wireless system. The built-in flash units on professional DSLRs such as the D3s and D700 can be used as the "*commander*" for a wireless setup, as can the SB-900 and SB-800 Speedlights. There is also a stand-alone commander—the SU-800. The SB-R200 Speedlight only works as part of such a system, not as a stand-alone flash, and Nikon uses this in its close-up flash system.

» FLASH ACCESSORIES

To add flexibility and control, a wide variety of flash accessories is available. Nikon has an extensive range, but when time is short (or money is tight) substitutes for some of these can be improvised.

Battery packs

Nikon produces add-on power packs for some of its Speedlights to speed up recycling times and extend battery life.

Color filters

Flash filters can be used to create striking color effects, or to match the color of the flash to that of the background lighting. Nikon produces various filters to fit its Speedlight range.

Flash cords

Also known as sync leads, these allow flashguns to be triggered when used off-camera. Dedicated cords such as Nikon's TTL Sync Cord SC-28 allow full communication between the camera and the Speedlight, retaining i-TTL flash control.

Flash diffusers

Flash diffusers are a simple and economical way of spreading and softening the hard light from a flash. Diffusers reduce the light reaching the subject (so the effective flash range will be shorter), but the D3100's metering system will allow for this when it determines the exposure. Diffusers may slide over the flash head in a similar fashion to Nikon's SW-13H diffusion dome (included with the SB-900), or attach by some other means. There are numerous options available, ranging from cheap, universal units designed to fit "any" flash, through to model-specific items such

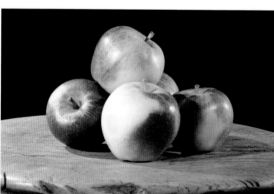

PAINTING WITH LIGHT 〈〈
This shot used four bursts of flash: one each from the left front, left rear, right front, and right rear.

ISO: 100
Focal Length: 105mm
Shutter Speed: 105 seconds
Aperture: f/16

as Sto-Fen's Omni-Bounce diffusers for hotshoe flashes and its Omni-Flip for built-in flash units such as the D3100's. A white handkerchief can be used at a pinch.

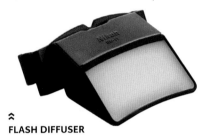

☆
FLASH DIFFUSER

Flash extenders

A flash extender is another simple accessory that slips over the flash head, using mirrors or a lens to create a tighter beam and therefore extend the effective range of the flash with longer lenses. Again, the D3100's metering system will automatically accommodate an extender, but as Nikon do not make flash-extenders, a third-party option will be required.

Flash brackets

The ability to mount the flash off-camera, and therefore change the angle at which the light hits the subject, is invaluable in controlling the quality of light. Nikon's Speedlights can be mounted on a tripod or stand on any flat surface using the AS-19 stand, but for a more portable solution many photographers prefer a light flexible

arm or bracket that attaches to the camera and supports the Speedlight. Novoflex produce a range of such products.

MULTIPLE FLASH UNITS ☆
The main flash was fired from the right rear, to backlight the bottles and create a glow. Further bursts of flash were added to light the background; from the side to give definition; and bounced off the ceiling to provide a fill.

ISO: 100
Focal Length: 80mm
Shutter Speed: 15 sec.
Aperture: f/16

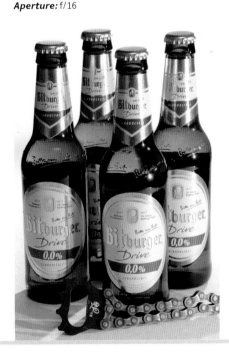

Chapter 5
CLOSE-UP

D3100

5   CLOSE-UP

Most photography is about capturing what you can see with the naked eye, but close-up photography goes beyond this, traveling into a whole new world—or at least a new way of seeing the world.

For close-up photography, a DSLR such as the D3100 is a great option, because reflex viewing—supplemented by Live View on occasions—is practically essential for close-up work. Also, the D3100 is part of the legendary Nikon system of lenses and accessories, which offers many additional options for close-up photography.

A key issue in close-up and macro photography is depth of field. As you move closer to the subject, the depth of field becomes narrower. This has several consequences. First, it is often necessary to stop down to small apertures, which can mean long exposures, and second, the slightest movement of either the subject or the camera can ruin the focus. For both reasons, a tripod or other solid camera support is often required, and it may be necessary to prevent the subject from moving also (within ethical limits!).

Because depth of field is so shallow, focusing becomes critical. Merely focusing on "the subject" is no longer adequate and you may have to decide which *part* of the subject—an insect's eye, or the stamen of

a flower, for example—should be the point of sharp focus. With its 11 focus points, the D3100 can focus accurately within much of the frame, but this is also where Live View mode comes into its own.

By selecting ⌷ᴶ **Wide-area AF** or ⌷ᴶ **Normal area AF**, the focus point can be set anywhere in the frame. If you prefer to use manual focus then Live View, with its zoomable view, makes this ultra-precise.

> ### Tip
>
> *To make sure that you're as close to the subject as you can possibly get, use manual focus and set the lens to its minimum focusing distance. Don't touch the focus control again. Instead move either the camera or the subject until the image is sharp. This may seem slow, but it guarantees that you're as close as the lens will allow.*

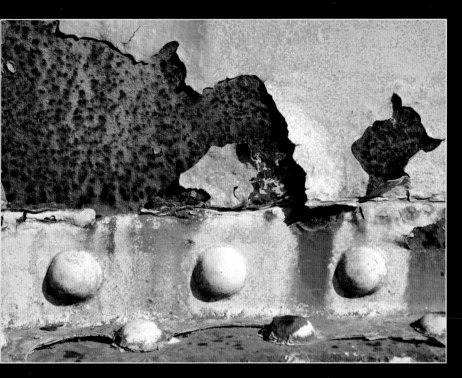

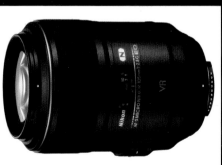

PEELING PAINT AND RIVETS ⌃
Close-up subjects are everywhere, and close-up photography really opens our eyes to them.

ISO: 320 *Focal Length:* 65mm
Shutter Speed: 1/640 sec. *Aperture:* f/11

NIKON MACRO LENS «

5 » MACRO PHOTOGRAPHY

There's no exact definition of "close-up" but the term "macro" really should be used more precisely. Macro photography traditionally means photography of objects at life-size or larger, implying that a true macro lens should allow a reproduction ratio of at least 1:1. Many zoom lenses are sold as having a "macro" capability when their reproduction ratio is around 1:4, or 1:2 at best. This still allows close-up photography, but it isn't macro by the classical definition.

Reproduction ratio

The reproduction ratio, or image magnification, is the ratio between the actual size of the subject and the size of its image on the D3100's imaging sensor. An object of the same dimensions captured at 1:1 would exactly fill the image frame. For example, an SD memory card is a little larger than the D3100's 23.6 x 15.8mm sensor, so at 1:1 the image of the card will completely fill the frame and then some. When the image is printed, or displayed on a computer screen, it may appear many times larger, but that's another story.

A 1:4 reproduction ratio (as seen on many so-called "macro" lenses) means that the smallest subject that would give you a frame-filling shot is one that's four times as long/wide as the sensor. With DX-format cameras such as the D3100 this is approximately 4 x 2 ½ inches (94 x 63mm), or slightly larger than a credit card.

Working distance

The working distance is the distance required to obtain the desired reproduction ratio with any given lens. It is related to the focal length of the lens: with a 200mm macro lens the working distance for 1:1 reproduction is double that of a 100mm focal length. Because the D3100's sensor is smaller than a 35mm film frame, the effective focal length of any lens is multiplied by approx 1.5x, and therefore working distance increases also. This extra distance can be valuable when photographing living subjects.

MACRO REPRODUCTION   »
The first shot *(top)* shows the closest view achieved with a "normal" 24–85mm zoom lens (approximately 1:2).

ISO: 250 *Focal Length:* 85mm Macro
Shutter Speed: 1/60 sec. *Aperture:* f/7.1

The second image *(bottom)* was taken with a 50mm macro lens at the closest possible distance, reproducing the frosted leaf at 1:1, or "life-size."

ISO: 250 *Focal Length:* 50mm Macro
Shutter Speed: 1/60 sec. *Aperture:* f/1.25

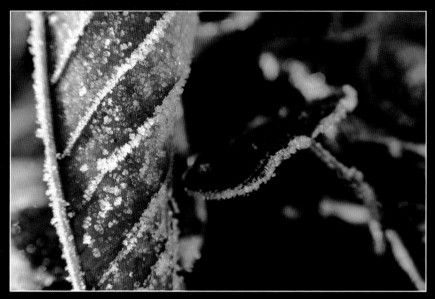

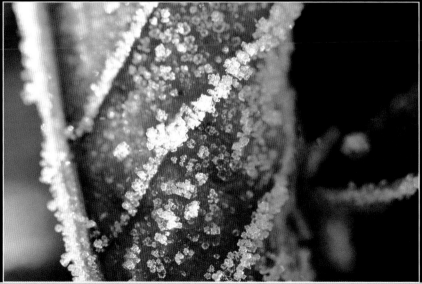

» EQUIPMENT FOR CLOSE-UP SHOOTING

Close-up attachment lenses

Close-up attachment lenses are simple magnifying lenses that screw into the filter thread of the lens. They are light, easy to carry and attach, and relatively inexpensive.

They are also easy to use as they are fully compatible with the camera's exposure and focusing systems. For best results, it's traditionally advised to use them with prime (fixed focal length) lenses.

Nikon produces six close-up attachment lenses:

Product number	Attaches to filter thread	Recommended for use with
0, 1, 2	52mm	Standard lenses
3T, 4T	52mm	Short telephoto lenses
5T, 6T	62mm	Telephoto lenses

› Extension tubes

Extension tubes (also known as extension rings) are another simple and relatively inexpensive means of extending the close-focusing capabilities of an existing lens. An extension tube is in essence a simple tube that fits between the lens and the camera. This decreases the minimum focusing distance and thereby increases the magnification factor. Extension tubes are light, compact, and easy to carry and attach, and because they contain no glass elements they should not compromise the optical quality of the lens. They can also be used with almost any lens.

The Nikon system includes four Extension tubes (PK-11A, PK-12, PK-13, and PN-11), which extend the lens by 8mm,

14mm, 27.5mm, and 52.5mm respectively. The PN-11 also incorporates a tripod mount. However, as the basic design of these tubes has not changed for many years, this means that some of the camera's functions are not available. In particular, there's no autofocus, although this is arguably less of a drawback in macro photography than in most other areas. On the D3100 these tubes must also be used in Manual (**M**) mode and the exposure determined by trial and error—but that's what playback and the histogram are for! If you're prepared to use the D3100 in a slightly "old-fashioned" way, they arguably offer the best low-cost introduction to true macro-photography.

Bellows

Bellows work on the same principle as extension tubes, by extending the spacing between the lens and the camera body, but are not restricted to a preset length. Again, there's no extra glass to impair the optical quality of the lens, but bellows are expensive, heavy, and cumbersome in comparison to extension tubes, and take time to set up. For these reasons, they are usually employed in controlled shooting situations, such as a studio.

Nikon's PB-6 bellows offers extensions from 48mm to 208mm, giving a maximum reproduction ratio of about 11:1. Focusing and exposure are manual only.

Reversing rings

Also known as reverse adaptors, or—in Nikon's jargon—"inversion rings," these allow lenses to be mounted in reverse; the adaptor screws into the filter thread. This allows much closer focusing than using the lens the "right" way round. Ideally used

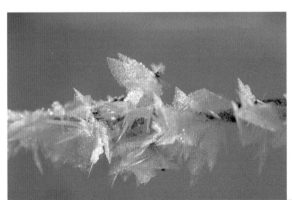

DEPTH OF FIELD   **«**
The minimal depth of field obtained in extreme close-up work is exemplified in this shot, at about 1:2 reproduction ratio. Focusing needs care, to ensure it falls exactly where it's wanted.

ISO: 200 *Focal Length:* 85mm
Shutter Speed: 1/400 sec.
Aperture: f/8

with a prime lens, a reversing ring could be coupled with an inexpensive, manual focus 50mm f/1.8. Nikon's Inversion ring BR-2A fits a 52mm filter thread.

> **Note:**
> Because accessories such as extension tubes and bellows increase the effective physical length of the lens, they also increase the effective focal length. However, the physical size of the aperture does not change. The result is that they make the lens "slower"; that is, a lens with a maximum aperture of f/2.8 starts to behave like an f/4 or f/5.6 lens. This makes the viewfinder image darker than normal, and affects the exposure required (although the camera's metering will compensate). Reversing rings do not have this effect.

Controlled lighting is often required for serious macro work, and this usually means flash. However, regular Speedlights are less than ideal. They are not designed for such close-range work and, if mounted on the hotshoe, the short working distance means that the lens may throw a shadow onto the subject. The built-in flash is even less suitable for real close-up work, with the Nikon manual suggesting it should not be used for subjects closer than 2ft (0.6m).

Specialist macro flash units usually take the form of either a ringflash or a twin flash, but because of the close operating distances they do not need high power so can be relatively light and compact.

Ringflash units fit round the lens itself, giving an even spread of light on ultra-close subjects (they're also favored by some portrait photographers). Nikon's

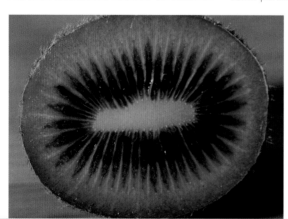

MACRO FLASH   **«**
This shot was produced with a minimal setup. Lighting was by a single flashgun to the left, with a reflector to the right to balance the light.

ISO: 200
Focal Length: 85mm
Shutter Speed: 1/80 sec.
Aperture: f/8

SB-29s has now been discontinued, but may still be found at some dealers. Alternatives can be found from Sigma and Marumi, amongst others.

Instead of ringflash, Nikon now concentrates on a twin-flash approach to close-up photography with its Speedlight Commander Kit R1C1 and Speedlight Remote Kit R1. These are both based around two Speedlight SB-R200 flashguns that mount either side of the lens. The R1C1 uses a Wireless Speedlight Commander SU-800 unit that fits into the camera's hotshoe, while the R1 uses a separate SB-900/SB-800 flash as the commander. These kits are expensive, but they do give very flexible and precisely controllable light for macro subjects.

› Improvisation

Dedicated macro-flashes aren't cheap, and may be unaffordable or unjustifiable for occasional macro work. Fortunately, there's a lot you can do with even the most basic—and cheap—flash, plus a remote cord. With the cheapest flash units you'll lose the D3100's advanced flash control,

but it only takes a few test shots to establish settings that you can use repeatedly.

Another essential is a small reflector—perhaps just a piece of white card—positioned as close as possible to the subject for maximum benefit. Used with a regular flash, this can be more flexible than twin-flash or ring-flash, allowing the light to be directed wherever you choose. On static subjects, "painting with light" is also an interesting option.

Tip

One reason why flash is often favored for close-up work is to overcome the problem of subject movement. When subject movement is due to breeze, it can be reduced using a "light tent," which also provides a diffused, even light on the subject. Proprietary examples are available from Lastolite, but it's possible to make your own; the trick is finding the right fabric, which needs to block the wind but let plenty of light through and be neutral in color.

True macro lenses achieve reproduction ratios of 1:1 or better and are optically optimized for close-up work, though they are normally very capable for general photography too. This is certainly true of Nikon's Micro Nikkor lenses, of which there are currently four.

AMBIENT AND FLASH LIGHTING ⌄

Obviously the flames themselves are a light source and I first took some test shots to establish the exposure that worked for these. I then added some flash from the left to light the candles, but shielded the background to make sure that it stayed dark.

ISO: 200 *Focal Length:* 85mm
Shutter Speed: 1/80 sec. *Aperture:* f/8

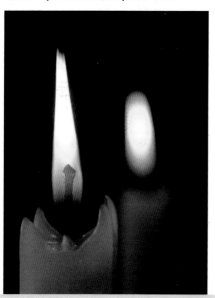

The 60mm f/2.8G ED AF-S Micro Nikkor uses ED (Extra-low dispersion) glass for superior optical quality, a Silent Wave Motor (SWM) for ultra-quiet autofocus, and a non-rotating front element, which makes life easier when using lens-mounted macro flashes.

The 105mm f/2.8G AF-S VR Micro Nikkor also features internal focusing, ED glass, and a Silent Wave Motor, and was also the world's first macro lens with VR (Vibration Reduction). As the slightest camera shake is magnified at high reproduction ratios, VR can be incredibly useful, allowing the use of shutter speeds as much as four stops slower than otherwise possible. However, it cannot compensate for subject movement.

The 200mm f/4D ED-IF AF Micro Nikkor is a particular favorite with those photographing the animal kingdom, as its longer working distance means there is much less chance of frightening your subject away. However, without a built-in focus motor it does not provide autofocus with the D3100.

TELEPHOTO MACRO LENSES »

Longer lenses are very useful for some subjects, especially ones that can fly away!

ISO: 400 *Focal Length:* 100mm
Shutter Speed: 1/200 sec. *Aperture:* f/11

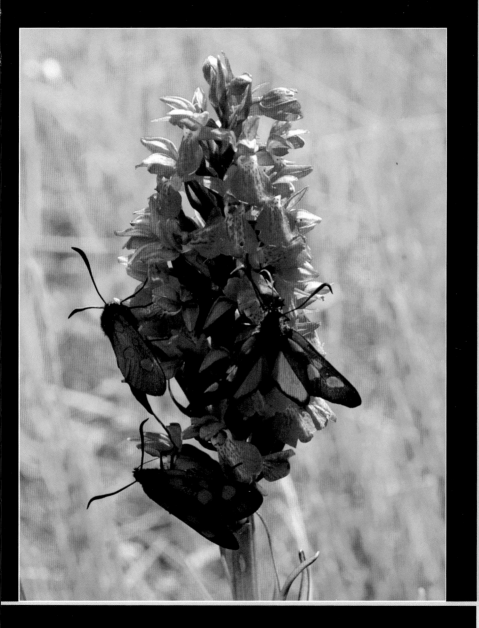

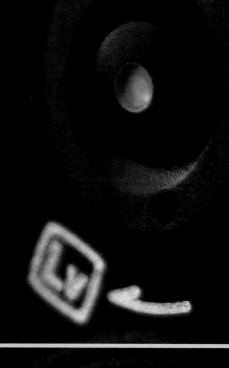

Chapter 6
MOVIES

6 MOVIES

The ability to record moving images is now widespread among DSLRs, but it was only as recently as 2008 that Nikon's D90 became the first DSLR from any manufacturer to offer this feature. Now, with the D3100, movie shooting is a feature across Nikon's entire DSLR range.

The movie mode is really an extension of Live View. This creates some idiosyncrasies and limitations, which need to be understood to get the best results. Familiarity with Live View shooting is a big asset when you start shooting movies.

Movie quality

The D3100 can shoot movies in Full HD (High Definition) quality with a frame size of 1920 x 1080 pixels. This naturally means that these movies can be played through an HD television, and will look excellent on most computer screens. The D3100 produces movies in a standard Motion-JPEG format (the file extension is AVI), which can be played through standard media players such as *QuickTime, RealPlayer*, and *Windows Media Player 9*.

Today, many compact cameras and camcorders also deliver HD resolution, but because the D3100 has a larger sensor, its image quality is superior in many respects. However, dedicated camcorders have ergonomic advantages.

The D3100 also allows you to select frame sizes of 1280 x 720 pixels and 640 x 424 pixels. This smallest size is adequate for

YouTube or playing on the majority of mobile devices, although the latest iPhones have a screen resolution of 960 x 640 pixels, and the iPad 1024 x 768 pixels. The lower settings allow you to record more video on the same memory card, so while a 4GB card will hold a little over 20 minutes of footage at the highest quality setting, almost two hours of footage can be recorded at the lowest quality setting.

Advantages

Although dedicated movie-makers will probably stick with cameras designed specifically for shooting video, the D3100 does have certain advantages. One of these is its ability to use the entire array of Nikon-fit lenses, giving a range that is difficult to match with any conventional video camera, especially for wide-angle shooting.

Another plus is that the D3100's larger sensor and ability to use lenses with wide maximum apertures means it is possible to achieve a very shallow depth of field, which is virtually unobtainable with compact cameras or camcorders. This can produce some very striking effects, and is one of the strongest features of the

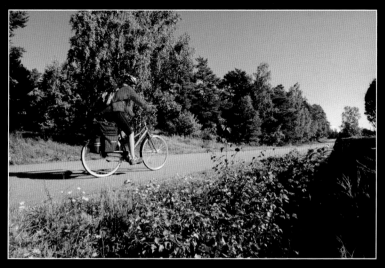

WIDE-ANGLE POTENTIAL ⌃
The D3100 allows wide-angle shooting.
Here a 12mm lens was used, giving a
strong foreground and plenty of room for
the rider to move through the scene.

LOW-LIGHT ADVANTAGE ⌄
The D3100 also scores when it comes to
low-light movie shooting.

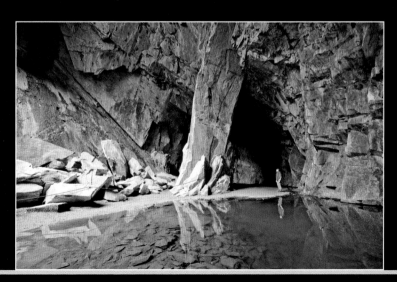

D3100's HD movie mode. The D3100's large sensor and high-ISO shooting ability also mean that results in low light should be better than most of the alternatives, while the full range of exposure settings, Picture Controls, and other options can be used to achieve a high level of creative control.

› Limitations

In terms of functionally, the D3100's movie mode is significantly more advanced than the D90, but some limitations remain. The viewing system makes handheld shooting awkward (the D5000, with its fold-out screen, has a slight edge here) while Live View AF isn't slick enough for fast-moving subjects. Sound quality from the built-in microphone is at best moderate, and you can't attach a separate microphone. There are also a few interesting image effects, as discussed below.

One other limitation is that you cannot record a single clip longer than 10 minutes, although for the viewer of your movies this is nearly always a good thing!

Image effects
The D3100, like other DSLRs, captures video using what is known as a "rolling" scan, which means the sensor is progressively exposed, rather than each frame being captured in one go. This

creates an unusual effect when dealing with fast movement, whether it's a rapid pan of the camera or movement of the subject itself—objects can appear distorted, with rectangular shapes turning to parallelograms and so on. If you rock the camera violently from side to side you can even achieve a remarkable wobbly effect that has become known as "jello-cam," although some editing software can now compensate for this.

Note:
Most digital video cameras claim enormous zoom ranges (often 800x or more), but these are only achieved by "digital zoom," which is a software function that enlarges the central portion of the image. Anything more than a small amount of digital zoom results in an obvious loss of image quality. The optical zoom range is what really matters, and the D3100's interchangeable lenses give a potential range of at least 50x (12–600mm). The widest focal-length range currently available in a single D3100-compatible lens is 18–270mm (from Tamron).

» SHOOTING MOVIES

Autofocus

The D3100 uses the same focusing options as Live View, including manual focus. While the quality of the Live View display makes manual focusing fairly easy (at least in good light), it is hard to operate the controls really smoothly, especially when handholding the camera.

Exposure

Exposure control depends on the exposure mode selected before shooting begins. If Auto or Scene modes are selected, exposure control is fully automatic, but in Scene modes the exposure level can be locked using the **AE-L/AF-L** button. This could be very useful if you want to prevent the main subject appearing to darken as it moves against a brighter background, for example.

If **P**, **A**, **S**, or **M** mode is selected, exposure levels can be adjusted by ±5EV using the ⊞ button and Command Dial. However, be aware that **A** and **M** modes create something of an illusion of manual control. In **A** mode, the Command Dial can be rotated during shooting and the aperture setting in the on-screen display will change accordingly, but the actual aperture in use does not change until the clip ends and you start shooting a new one. The only way to adjust exposure mid-shot is with the ⊞ button and Command Dial together: in **M** mode you can't even do this. So, while these modes may still be useful, you need to remember that you are limited to setting the exposure *before* you start recording.

While all these adjustment options are welcome, actually using them while

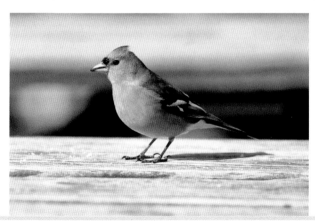

DSLR DEPTH OF FIELD «
It's much easier to get a really shallow depth of field with a DSLR than with most dedicated video cameras.

6

shooting is fiddly. It's difficult to avoid shaking the camera unless it's on a very solid tripod, and the built-in microphone can also pick up the sounds you make as you handle the camera. Another consequence can be abrupt changes in brightness levels in the resulting footage. Getting these things right takes practice!

Sound

The D3100 has a built-in microphone that provides modest-quality mono output. The internal mic is very sensitive to wind noise and is also liable to pick up any sounds you make while operating the camera (focusing, zooming, and even breathing). Older lenses may have noisy AF motors, too, and while AF-S lenses with their Silent Wave motors are much quieter, they are still not completely silent. The Movie settings section of the Shooting menu includes the option to turn the microphone off if this is a problem.

Turning the microphone off makes sense if you plan to add a new soundtrack later, and adding a music track or separate, scripted commentary is straightforward. However, this is not ideal if you want to record specific ambient sounds, and harder still if you want to include people speaking. If you need to include dialog or "talking heads," keep your subjects close to the camera and ensure that any background

noise is minimized while you shoot—it is best not to fiddle with the camera while recording speech, so set everything you need to before you start.

Preparation

Before starting to shoot, select your key settings in the **Movie settings** section of the Shooting menu. This has two sub-menus: Quality, and Sound.

Quality sets the image size, frame rate, and quality for movie recording. The size options are: **640 x 424** pixels (default), **1920 x 1080** pixels, and **1280 x 720** pixels. The frame-rate options vary according to the image size and whether PAL or NTSC is selected as the video mode.

Sound simply turns the built-in microphone **ON** or **OFF**.

Shooting video clips

1) Choose the exposure mode, AF mode, and AF-area mode as you would for Live View shooting.

2) Activate Live View by flicking the **LV** switch on the back of the camera.

3) Check framing and initial exposure level. If using **A** or **M** exposure mode, set the aperture. Set initial focus by half-pressure on the shutter-release button.

4) Press ●**Rec** (center of the Live View switch) to start recording the movie. **REC** flashes in red at the top of the screen while recording, and an indicator shows the remaining shooting time.

5) To stop recording, press ●**Rec** again.

6) Exit Live View by flicking the **LV** switch.

CAMERA MOVEMENTS ⨯
This looks like a simple shot, but in the deep snow it wasn't possible to get far enough back off the trail for a true panning shot. This shot required zooming out as the team and sled passed, while relying on the camera to follow focus.

Tip

To take a still photo during movie shooting, press the shutter-release button and keep it pressed until you hear the shutter operate. Still frames can also be extracted from movies, but will only be at the image size selected for movie recording.

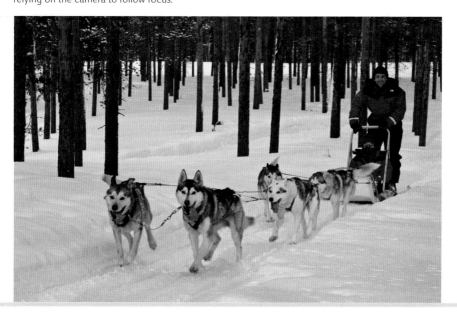

A golden rule when shooting movies with the D3100, even more than stills, is to think ahead. If you shoot a still frame and it isn't quite right, you can review it, change position or settings, and be ready to shoot again within a second or two. To shoot and review even a short movie clip eats up much more time, and often you don't get a second chance. Therefore, it's doubly important to make sure your shooting position, framing, and camera settings are right before you start. It's easy to check the general look of the shot by shooting a still frame before you start the movie clip; this is a good habit to get into.

However, a still frame does not allow for movement of the subject, the camera, or both. For example, the D3100 has limited ability to follow focus on a moving subject in movie shooting. This can be an issue if your subject is moving toward or away from the camera, or you plan to pan across a scene that contains objects at a range of different distances. You can sometimes rely on the depth of field to cope with this (more so when shooting with wide-angle lenses than long telephotos), but rapid subject movement can be a real problem.

As this suggests, it is relatively easy to shoot action when the subject is at a constant distance (for example, panning shots from the inside of a curve), but if it isn't, you'll need to make sure you have a sufficient depth of field, so use a small aperture and be prepared to set a high ISO setting if necessary.

Shooting movies is plainly more complex than shooting stills, so it makes sense to start with simple shots; don't try zooming, panning, *and* changing focus simultaneously when you start out—adjust one thing at a time. Many moving subjects can be filmed with a fixed camera; examples include waterfalls, birds at a feeder, musicians playing, and many more. Equally, you can become familiar with camera movement while shooting static subjects: try panning across a wide landscape or zooming in from a broad cityscape to a detail of a single building.

Handheld or tripod shooting
Shooting movie clips handheld is a good way to reveal just how wobbly you really are—especially as you can't use the viewfinder—but even "real" movie directors sometimes use a handheld camera to create a specific feel. This was done to great effect in the film *Cloverfield,* but would you really want every movie clip you shoot to look like that? There's a big difference between controlled wobble for deliberate effect, and uncontrolled shakiness. Using a tripod, or other suitable camera support, is the easiest way to give your movie clips a polished, professional

look, and this is not only true for static shots, but even more so when you start panning or zooming.

If you choose to handhold the camera, or need to shoot a clip with no tripod available, approach it carefully. Pick a spot where you won't be jostled and look for solid support for your elbows—by sitting with your elbows braced on your knees, for example. Whatever you do, "think steady."

Tip

A standard tripod with a pan-and-tilt head is a good start for DSLR movie shooting, assuming it's fairly stable. The alternative ball-and-socket heads are fine for static shots and zooms, but far less suitable for panning. If you're serious about movies, consider investing in a dedicated video tripod. This isn't necessarily bigger or heavier than its standard photographic counterpart, but the tripod head is specifically designed for smooth movements. The best are fluid-damped for ultra-smooth results, and you may well find that your existing tripod legs can still be used so you only need to change the tripod head.

› Panning

The panning shot is a mainstay of movie making. Often essential for following a moving subject, it can also be used to great effect with static subjects. For instance, a panning shot enables you to capture a vast panorama in a way that's impossible in a static shot or still frame. Handheld panning is hard to get right; it may look acceptable when following a moving subject, but a wobbly pan across a grand landscape will grate on most viewers. This really does call for a tripod.

The tripod must be properly leveled, though, otherwise you may start panning with the camera aimed at the horizon but finish with it showing nothing but the ground or sky. Many tripods have a built-in spirit level, but you can easily check that the tripod's center-column looks vertical from all sides, or do a "dry-run" before shooting. If you're panning to follow a moving subject you also need to think about the subject's expected path. Some subjects move along predictable paths—trains and trams being obvious examples—but at the other extreme, trying to follow a player in a soccer match can be very challenging, and even seasoned pros don't always get it right.

The best place to start practicing your panning shots is on static subjects such as landscapes. Of course, landscapes aren't always static, and the combination of a panning shot with waves breaking on the shore, running water, or grass blowing in the breeze can produce beautiful results.

Keep panning movements slow and steady, as panning too rapidly can make it hard to "read" the shot and even make the viewer feel seasick. On the D3100 it can also make objects appear distorted. Smooth panning is easiest with video tripods, but perfectly possible with a standard model: leave the pan adjustment slack, but make sure the other adjustments are tight. It is better to hold the tripod head, rather than the camera, and it can also be easier if you don't try and look at the screen as you pan, which should be unnecessary if you've framed the shot properly in advance. Instead, use the front of the lens as a reference to track steadily across the scene.

With moving subjects, the speed and direction of panning is dictated by the need to keep the subject in frame. Here, you may need to watch the screen in order to keep the subject in approximately the same place in the frame, although fast-moving subjects can still be very hard to track accurately. They can also end up looking distorted, but as this is an inherent limitation of video capture with a DSLR, you either have to accept it or look for slower subjects.

> ## Tip

Many tripod heads have projecting arms that are used to lock and unlock the movements; one of these controls the pan adjustment and holding this lightly at its end helps to get a smooth, even panning movement. Extra length gives even finer control, so consider adding an extension, even if it's something improvised.

> ## Zooming

The zoom is another fundamental movie technique. Moving from a wide view to a tighter one is called *zooming in*, and the converse is *zooming out*. A little forethought makes all the difference to using the zoom effectively, so consider which zoom direction you want, and think about the framing of the shot both at the start and at the end. If you're zooming in to a specific subject, double-check it's central to the frame before your start.

The D3100 and its range of available lenses are not designed specifically for shooting movies and this shows up clearly when it comes to zooming. First, none of them have such a wide zoom range as video camera lenses, although

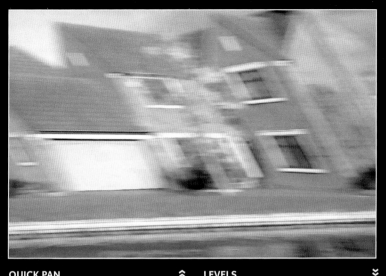

QUICK PAN ⌃
A too-rapid pan can make objects appear distorted due to the "rolling" shutter used by the D3100 (and other DSLRs) when it records movies.

LEVELS ⌄
Panning with the cyclist is an obvious shot, but the tripod needs to be leveled correctly in advance, or the streets of Copenhagen could appear to be far from level!

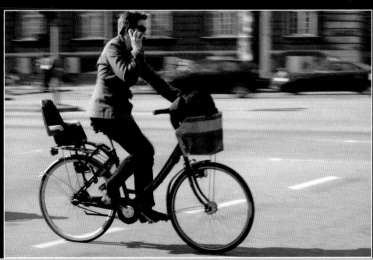

"superzooms" such as Tamron's 18–270mm can be useful for movie shooting. They may lack ultimate quality for still images, but video (even Full HD) has much lower definition requirements. Even so, you may sometimes have to cut from one shot to another instead of linking them in a continuous zoom.

Second, it's hard to achieve a totally smooth, even-paced zoom action. Practice helps, and firmly mounting the camera on a solid tripod helps even more, but zooming while handholding the camera guarantees a jerky zoom action and overall wobbliness. If you have several lenses available, it's worth experimenting to see which has the smoothest zoom action.

A really quick zoom, known as a "whip zoom," is very hard to execute properly with most lenses on the D3100, but you can try. It can always be edited out later, replacing the zoom with a quick "cut" from the wide shot to close-up: running the camera for a few seconds before and after the zoom will give you enough "static" footage to use for this purpose.

When zooming, remember that depth of field decreases at the telephoto end of the range, so your subject may appear perfectly sharp in a wide-angle view, but end up looking quite fuzzy when you zoom in. If the camera refocuses, the sudden shift in focus is itself a distraction. To avoid this, set the focus manually at the telephoto end of the zoom, regardless of whether this is the starting point for a zoom out, or the end of a zoom in.

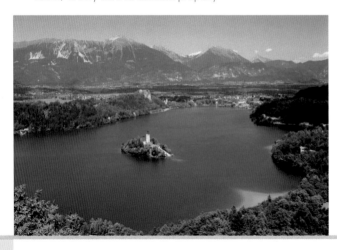

EXPLORING THE SCENE «
The camera can "explore" a scene like this either by panning across it or by zooming in.

» FOCUSING

The D3100 will try and automatically maintain focus while movie recording is in progress, provided Full-time servo AF (**AF-F**) is selected, although it may lag behind rapid camera movements. If Single-servo AF (**AF-S**) is selected, the camera will only refocus when you half-press the shutter-release button, and this is often all too obvious in the final movie clip. However, keeping half-pressure on the button is one way of locking focus and it is perfectly viable to use a fixed-focus distance for each shot, especially when the depth of field is good. This reduces operations that can make the shot wobbly and avoids distracting focus shifts.

Manual focusing is also possible, but can be another recipe for wobbly pictures. Once again, this necessitates the use of a tripod, especially with longer lenses where the focusing is more critical and any

movement will be magnified. Some lenses may have a smoother manual-focus action than others, and the physical design of older lenses often makes them more suitable, thanks to their large, well-placed focus rings. Older lenses also tend to have a distance scale marked on the lens barrel, which can offer an alternative to using the Live View display to focus, while pre-focusing manually also avoids undesirable focus shifts during shooting.

Study the credits for major movies and TV shows and you'll often see someone called a "focus puller." This is an assistant to the camera operator, whose sole task is to adjust the focus, normally between predetermined points (for instance shifting from one character's face to another). This leaves the lead camera operator free to concentrate on framing, panning, and zooming. Frequently, the focus puller uses the distance scale on the lens barrel, relying on previously measured distances. While this may seem a far cry from shooting simple movie clips on the D3100, it does suggest that it could be worth trying a bit of teamwork, especially if you want to pan or zoom at the same time as adjusting focus.

Warning!

Older lenses (any lens lacking a CPU) can only be used on the D3100 in Manual mode, and exposure setting is by trial and error. This can be done fairly quickly by shooting a few still frames and checking the histogram, so such lenses may still be worth using, if only for their smooth focusing action.

Importing movies to the computer

The basic procedure for importing movies is much the same as for stills. *Nikon Transfer* will recognize and import your video clips, but importing your movie files through movie-editing software is often preferable—it ensures all your movie clips are stored in the same place so the software can immediately locate them for editing.

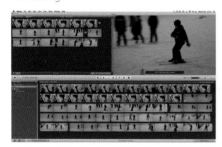

Apple's iMovie ⌃

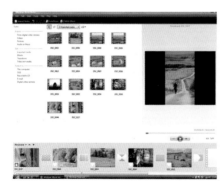

Windows Movie Maker ⌃

Like all movie cameras, the D3100 doesn't shoot movies; it shoots movie *clips*. A single clip straight from the camera may serve for some purposes, but to turn a collection of clips into a movie that people actually want to see requires editing.

The name of the game here is non-linear editing (NLE). This simply means that the clips in the final movie don't have to appear in the same order in which they were shot: you might shoot a stunning tropical sunset on the first night of your holiday, for example, but use it as the closing shot in your movie.

With modern software, editing movies is almost easier to do than it is to describe, especially as the D3100's AVI clips are a standard format that can be edited in most available programs. Even better, if you own a reasonably recent computer you probably already have suitable software installed with the operating system.

For Mac users, the obvious choice is Apple's *iMovie*, part of the *iLife* suite, which is included with all new Macs. The Windows equivalent is *Windows Movie Maker*, which came pre-installed with Windows Vista, but needs to be downloaded from www.windowslive.com if you're using Windows 7.

Both programs offer non-linear editing, and it's also *non-destructive*. This just means that editing does not affect your original clips (unlike cutting and splicing bits of film in the "old days"). The editing software works by copying the desired sections of your clips and keeping "notes" on the edit. This means that during the editing process you are working with preview versions of your video footage and a new movie file is only created when you select **Export Movie** (in *iMovie*) or **Save** (in *Windows Movie Maker*).

The two programs work in broadly similar ways, and both are easy to grasp. *iMovie* has a largely visual interface, while *Windows Movie Maker* relies slightly more on text-based menus, but in both cases the movie clips you work with are displayed in one pane of the screen and you simply drag the one you want to the **Project** pane *(iMovie)* or **Timeline** *(Windows Movie Maker)* to use it. You can rearrange your clips at any time just by "dragging-and-dropping," and you can also trim each

clip to a desired length. A **Viewer** window allows you to preview your movie as a work-in-progress at any time.

In addition, you can adjust the look of any clip or segment of the movie. There are basic controls for brightness, color, and so on (as with a photo-editing program), and a range of special effects can be added. You can, for example, make your movie look "aged" (scratched and faded), as if it had been shot 50 years ago on film, rather than yesterday using your DSLR.

Another basic feature is the *transition*. This means that instead of simply cutting instantaneously from one shot to the next, you can apply various effects such as dissolves, wipes, and fades. These are fun to play with and can add visual polish to the finished movie, but should enhance the shots either side and help the narrative flow of the movie, rather than calling attention to themselves. It's generally better to work with just a few transitions rather than using every possible option in the course of a five-minute movie.

Adding to your movie

Apple's *iMovie* and *Windows Movie Maker* both allow you to add other media to your movie, such as still photos and sound. With a quality camera like the D3100, adding stills is a natural and easy thing to do, but you can also use photos from other

---

Tip

It's fun to play with special effects, and non-destructive editing means you can experiment to your heart's content. But it's best to use them sparingly in the final version if you want audiences to enjoy, rather than endure, your movie.

6

sources. You can insert them individually at appropriate points, or create slideshows within the main movie. Again, various effects and transitions can be applied to give a more dynamic feel as you move from one photo to the next, but it is best not to overuse these.

It's equally easy to add a new soundtrack, such as a voiceover or music, to part (or all) of the movie, and the limitations of the camera's built-in microphone often make this desirable.

Finally, you could add titles and captions—perhaps crediting yourself as producer, director, camera operator, sound recordist, editor, "best boy," and/or key grip!

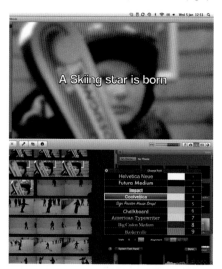

Adding titles in iMovie ⌃

Storyboarding

Editing can transform a jumbled assortment of movie clips into a coherent movie, but it can also lead to frustration when you start to wish you had a wider shot of X, or a close-up of Y. Editing can do a lot, but it can't supply footage that you didn't record in the first place. This is where planning comes in, and is the primary reason why a lot of big movie productions start with a storyboard, before a single scene is shot. This typically looks like a giant comic strip, with sketches or mock-ups of every shot and scene that's envisaged in the final movie. Things can still change significantly in the final edit, but storyboarding helps make sure that the director and editor have all the material they need to work with. You may not want to go quite that far with your own movie projects, but the more you can plan ahead, the better.

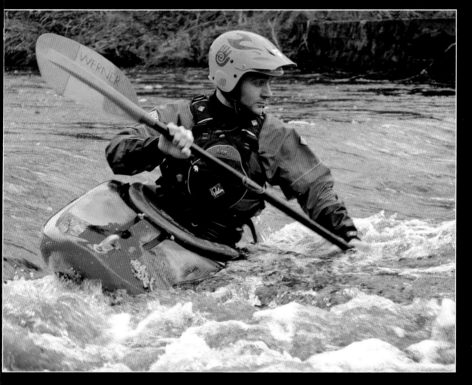

FRAMING ⌃
Playing in a standing wave, this kayaker remained in roughly the same place for several minutes, making it easy to keep him in the frame.

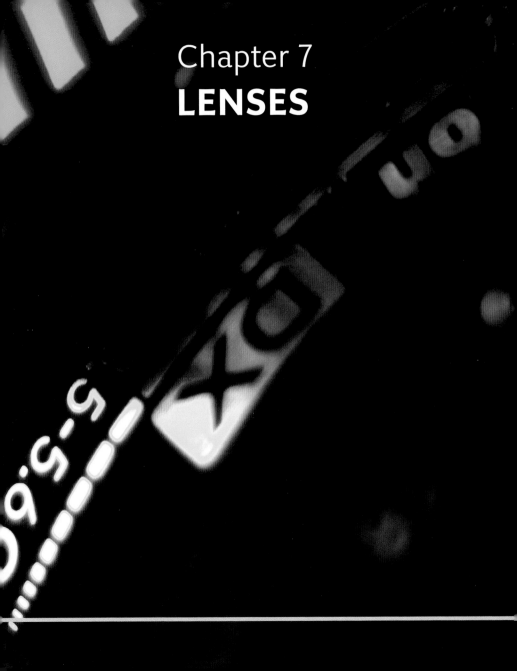

Chapter 7
LENSES

7 LENSES

There are many reasons for choosing a DSLR such as the D3100 over a digital compact camera, but one of the most important is the ability to use a vast range of lenses.

Whether it's a lens from Nikon's own legendary system or a lens from another manufacturer, Nikon's F-mount—in its basic form—is 50 years old. The philosophy of continuity of the lens-mount design means that most Nikkor lenses will fit the D3100, and work (although sometimes with major limitations). However, there are still sound reasons why the best lenses for this digital camera are among the more recent range.

One of the most obvious disadvantages is that many older lenses will not allow autofocus on the D3100, simply because autofocus had not been developed when they were designed.

Another reason for preferring lenses designed specifically for digital cameras relates to the way in which light reaches the individual photodiodes or "photosites" on the camera's sensor. Because these are slightly recessed, there can be some cut-off if light hits them at an angle. This was less critical with 35mm film, for which older Nikkor lenses were designed, but Nikon's DX-series and other newer lenses are specifically designed to ensure that light hits the sensor as perpendicular as possible to maintain illumination and image quality across the (digital) frame.

While many older lenses can still be used (and will often give very good results), critical examination may show some loss of brightness toward the edges of the frame, and perhaps a hint of chromatic aberration (color fringing). Wide-angle lenses are most susceptible, telephotos less so, although much depends on the size of print or reproduction you require. These shortcomings can to some extent be corrected in post-processing (especially if you shoot RAW files), but all DX lenses are specifically designed for digital cameras and will therefore largely avoid such problems to start with.

Loss of functions

When older lenses are used on the Nikon D3100, many functions may be lost, and autofocus is only available with lenses that have a built-in motor: suitable Nikon lenses are designated AF-I or AF-S, but check carefully when considering older lenses from independent makers. Other AF lenses with a built-in CPU will support some or all of the camera's metering functions and exposure modes, but will require focusing manually. The electronic rangefinder can be helpful here.

Older lenses without a built-in CPU, such as Nikon's AI and AI-S types, can be attached, but none of the camera's metering modes will operate. It is therefore necessary to focus manually and use Manual exposure (**M**) also. You can set the aperture and shutter speed by using an external meter, or simply through trial and error, possibly using the histogram as a guide to getting the correct exposure. This might seem like a lot of trouble, but it rarely takes more than a minute, and could be well rewarded if, for

example, you have an old 50mm AI lens: used with a reversing ring this would be an inexpensive but excellent solution for macro photography, for example.

Warning!

Some older lenses—specifically pre-AI lenses—should not be used as damage can result. Non-AI lenses can be recognized by their distinctive meter-coupling prong (see photo). Certain other specific (and uncommon) lenses should also be avoided—see the D3100's manual for further details.

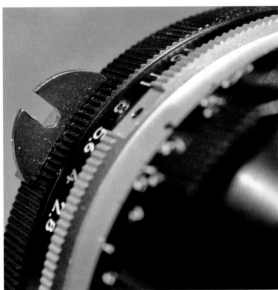

The distinctive meter »
coupling of a pre-AI lens.

7 » NIKON LENS TECHNOLOGY

Nikon's lens range has long been renowned for its technical and optical excellence, and many of the company's modern lenses incorporate special features or materials. These lenses are referred to extensively in the tables on pages 219–221, so here is a brief explanations of the main terms and acronyms used.

ABBREVIATION	TERM	EXPLANATION
AF	Autofocus	Lens focuses automatically. The majority of current Nikkor lenses are AF, but a substantial manual focus range remains.
ASP	Aspherical Lens Elements	Precisely configured lens elements that reduce the incidence of certain aberrations. Especially useful in helping to reduce distortion with wide-angle lenses.
CRC	Close-range Correction	Advanced lens design that improves picture quality at close focusing distances.
D	Distance information	Type D and Type G lenses communicate information to the camera about the distance at which they are focusing, supporting functions such as 3D Matrix Metering II.
DC	Defocus-image Control	Found in a few lenses aimed at portrait photographers. Allows control of aberrations and thereby the appearance of out-of-focus areas in the image.
DX	DX lens	Lenses specifically designed for DX-format digital cameras such as the D3100.
G	G-Type lens	Modern Nikkor lenses with no aperture ring; aperture must be set by the camera
ED	Extra-low Dispersion glass	ED glass minimizes chromatic aberration (the tendency for light of different colors to be focused at slightly different points).

ABBREVIATION	TERM	EXPLANATION
IF	Internal Focusing	Only internal elements of the lens move during focusing, meaning the front element does not extend or rotate.
M/A	Manual/Auto	Most Nikkor AF lenses offer M/A mode, which allows the seamless transition from automatic to manual focusing if required.
N	Nano Crystal Coat	Said to virtually eliminate internal reflections within lenses, guaranteeing minimal flare.
PC	Perspective Control	See p217.
RF	Rear Focusing	Lens design where only the rearmost elements move during focusing, which makes AF operation faster.
SIC	Super Integrated Coating	Nikon-developed lens coating that minimizes flare and "ghosting."
SWM	Silent Wave Motor	Special in-lens motors that deliver very fast and very quiet autofocus operation.
VR	Vibration Reduction	System that compensates for camera shake. VR is said to allow handheld shooting up to three stops slower than would otherwise be possible, so a shutter speed of 1/15 sec. could be used instead of 1/125 sec. New lenses feature VRII, said to offer a gain of an additional stop over VR (allowing a shutter speed of 1/8 sec. to be used instead of 1/125 sec., for example).

7 » FOCAL LENGTH

Most photographers are familiar with the term "focal length," but it is often misapplied. The focal length of any lens is a basic optical characteristic, and it is not changed by fitting the lens to a different camera. A 20mm lens is a 20mm lens, no matter what. Unfortunately the lenses on most digital compact cameras are described not by their actual focal length but by their "35mm equivalent," which is the focal length that would give the same angle of view on a 35mm or full-frame (FX-format) camera.

Of course, zoom lenses have a variable focal length—that's what zoom means—but an 18-55mm zoom possesses an 18-55mm focal length, regardless of whether it is mounted on a DX-format camera such as the D3100, or fitted to an FX format camera such as the D3s.

Crop factor

The D3100's smaller sensor means that it has a crop factor (also referred to as *focal length magnification factor*) of 1.5x, so if you fit a 200mm lens to a D3100, the field of view is equivalent to a 300mm lens on a full-frame camera (D3, D3x or D700). For sports and wildlife this can be an advantage, allowing long-range shooting with relatively light and inexpensive lenses. However, at the same time, the crop factor means that wide-angle lenses effectively become less wide, which is not such good news for landscape shooters. One consequence has been the development of ultra-wide lenses, such as the 14mm f/2.8D ED AF Nikkor—a 21mm focal length equivalent when fitted to the D3100.

Field of view

The field of view, or angle of view, is the area covered by the image frame. While the focal length of a lens remains the same on any camera, the angle of view seen in the image is different for different sensor formats. The angle of view is usually measured diagonally (as in the tables on pages 219-221).

Perspective

Perspective concerns the visual relationship between objects at different distances. The apparent fading of distant objects due to haze or the scattering of light is known as *atmospheric perspective*, while *optical perspective* refers to changes in the apparent size of objects at different distances. It's commonly asserted that different focal lengths produce a different

A series of images taken on a Nikon D3100, from a fixed position, with focal lengths of 12–300mm.

ISO: 160
Shutter Speed: 1/125 sec. *Aperture:* f/11

Focal Length: 12mm

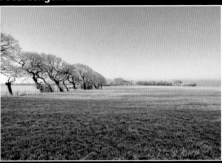

Focal Length: 17mm

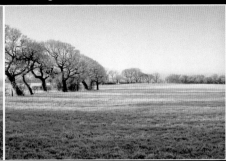

Focal Length: 24mm

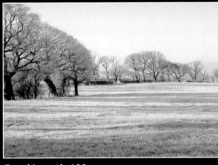

Focal Length: 50mm

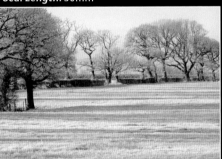

Focal Length: 100mm

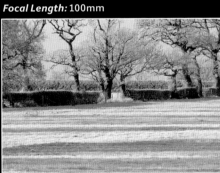

Focal Length: 200mm

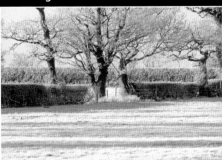

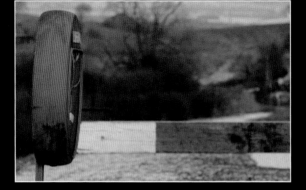

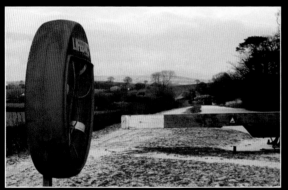

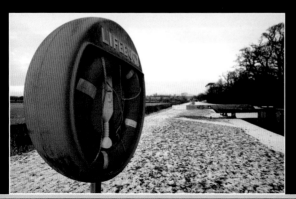

POINT OF VIEW **«**
These three images were taken
using, 200mm (*top*), 50mm
(*center*), and 12mm (*bottom*)
focal lengths, moving the
camera position so that the
main subject remained the
same size in the frame. Note
how the background appears
to change.

perspective, but this is wrong: perspective is determined solely by distance. However, as different lenses do lend themselves to different working distances they are often associated with different perspectives.

A powerful emphasis on the foreground may be loosely called "wide-angle perspective," because a wide-angle lens allows you to move closer to foreground objects. Similarly, the apparent compression of perspective in telephoto shots is a result of the greater working distance associated with the long lens. In the series of shots facing, the lifering remains the same apparent size even though it's viewed from different distances, but both its apparent shape and its relationship to the background are altered.

› Standard lenses

In traditional 35mm film photography, a 50mm lens was called "standard" because its field of view approximated that of the human eye. Because of the crop factor of the D3100, the equivalent lens would be around 35mm. Fixed focal length (or "prime") standard lenses are typically light, simple, and have wide maximum apertures. Zoom lenses whose range includes the 35mm focal length are often referred to as "standard zooms."

STANDARD LENS ⏬
The standard lens is versatile enough to be used for a variety of subjects.

ISO: 100 *Focal Length:* 35mm
Shutter Speed: 1/250 sec. *Aperture:* f/10

50mm f/1.4G AF-S "standard" lens ⏬

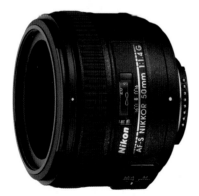

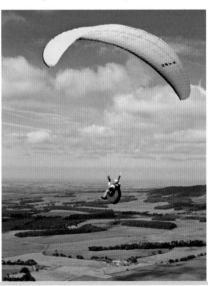

› Wide-angle lenses

A wide-angle lens is any lens with a wider view than a standard lens; for the D3100 this means any focal length shorter than 35mm. Wide-angle lenses are valuable when you want to work close to your subject or bring foregrounds into greater prominence. They lend themselves both to photographing expansive scenic views and to working in cramped spaces where it isn't possible to step back to "get more in."

Because of the D3100's crop factor, a lens such as a 17mm—once regarded as "super-wide"—gives a less extreme angle of view, boosting demand for a new breed of lenses, such as Nikon's 12–24mm f/4G ED-IF AF-S DX zoom.

12–24mm f/4G ED-IF AF-S DX zoom ⌄

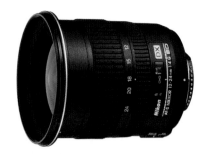

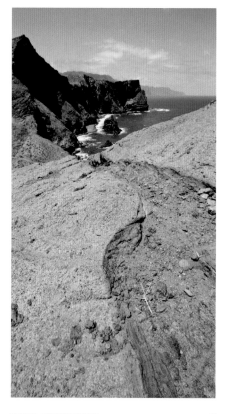

WIDE-ANGLE LENS ⌃
Wide-angle lenses don't just add width, but also enhance the third dimension: depth.

ISO: 400
Focal Length: 12mm
Shutter Speed: 1/250 sec.
Aperture: f/14

› Telephoto lenses

Telephoto lenses, often simply called "long lenses," give a narrow angle of view. They are mostly employed where working distances need to be longer, as in wildlife and sports photography, but have many other uses, such as singling out small and/or distant elements in a landscape.

Moderate telephoto lenses are favored for portrait photography because the greater working distance gives a natural-looking result and is more comfortable for the subject. The traditional "portrait" range is an 85-135mm focal length, equivalent to 60-90mm with the D3100.

The laws of optics, plus a greater working distance, mean that telephoto lenses produce a limited depth of field. This is often beneficial for portraiture, wildlife, and sports, as it concentrates attention on the subject by throwing the background out of focus, but it can be less welcome in landscape shooting.

The size and weight of longer lenses makes them harder to handhold comfortably, and their narrow angle of view also magnifies any movement; fast shutter-speeds and/or the use of a tripod or other camera support are therefore the order of the day. Nikon's Vibration Reduction (VR) technology also helps mitigate the effects of camera shake.

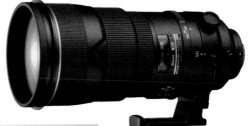

300mm f/4D ED-IF AF-S ≪

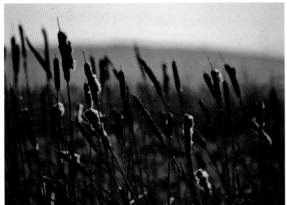

TELEPHOTO LENS　≪
The long working distances associated with telephoto lenses creates compressed perspectives.

ISO: 200
Focal Length: 200mm
Shutter Speed: 1/2000 sec.
Aperture: f/5.6

› Zoom lenses

The term "zoom" is used for lenses with a variable focal length, such as the AF-S DX Nikkor 18–105mm f/3.5-5.6G ED VR. It's easy to see that a zoom lens can replace a bagful of prime lenses and cover the gaps in between. Therefore, zoom lenses score highly for weight, convenience, and economy, and their flexible focal length also allows the very precise framing of images. While they were once considered inferior in terms of optical quality, there is now little to choose between a good zoom and a good prime lens. That said, cheaper zooms, and those with a very wide focal length range (18–200mm or 28–300mm, for example) may still be optically compromised, and usually have a relatively small ("slow") maximum aperture.

18–105mm f/3.5-5.6G ED AF-S VR DX ⌄

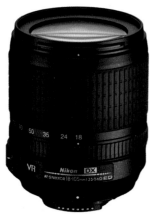

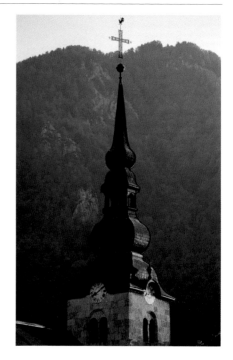

ZOOM LENS ⌃
Zoom lenses are a real advantage when precise framing is required.

ISO: 250 *Focal Length:* 95mm
Shutter Speed: 1/250 sec. *Aperture:* f/4.5

› Macro lenses

For specialist close-up work there is little to beat a true macro lens: for more on these *see page 184.*

› Perspective control lenses

Perspective control (or *tilt and shift*) lenses give unique flexibility in viewing and controlling the image. Their most obvious, but by no means only, value is in photographing architecture. With a "normal" lens it often becomes necessary to tilt the camera upward to fit the building in frame, which results in converging verticals, where buildings appear to lean back or even to one side.

The shift function of a perspective control (PC) lens allows the camera-back to be kept vertical, which in turn means that vertical lines in the subject remain vertical in the image, as shown below.

The current Nikon range features three PC lenses, with focal lengths of 24mm, 45mm, and 85mm. They retain many automatic functions, but all are manual focus lenses.

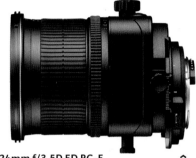

24mm f/3.5D ED PC–E

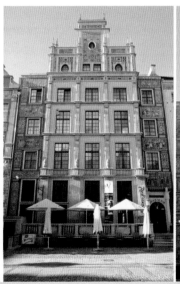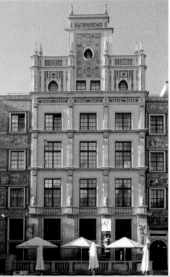

PERSPECTIVE «
CONTROL LENS
Converging verticals were all too obvious in the first, uncorrected version of this shot.

ISO: 320
Focal Length: 24mm
Shutter Speed: 1/60 sec.
Aperture: f/13

Teleconverters are supplementary optics that fit between the lens and the camera body, magnifying the focal length. Nikon currently offers three models, the TC-14E II, TC-17E II, and TC-20E II, giving magnifications of 1.4x, 1.7x, and 2x respectively. So, using a TC-17E II on a 50mm prime lens would effectively make it an 85mm focal length (equivalent to 127.5mm on the D3100 when the crop

factor is taken into account). The advantages are obvious—teleconverters allow you to extend your available focal length range relatively cheaply and with minimal additional weight (the TC-14E II, for example, weighs just 200 grams).

However, there's no such thing as a free lunch; teleconverters tend to degrade image quality slightly and also cause a loss of light that may mean the camera's autofocus can become sluggish or even totally unresponsive.

Lens hoods

A lens hood has two main functions: it helps to protect the lens against knocks, rain, and so on, and it helps to exclude stray light that may degrade the image by causing flare. Most Nikkor lenses come with a dedicated lens hood.

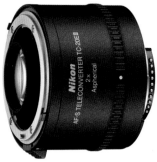

Teleconverter ☆

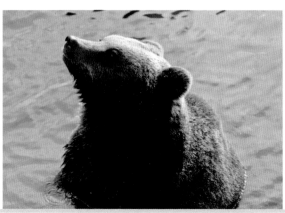

EXTENDING THE FOCAL LENGTH »
A teleconverter can save the weight and cost of a separate "long" lens.
ISO: 400
Focal Length: 160mm
Shutter Speed: 1/640 sec.
Aperture: f/4

» NIKKOR LENS CHARTS

The following tables list currently available Nikkor lenses, starting with the DX-series lenses that are specifically designed for DX format cameras such as the D3100.

	Optical features / notes	Angle of view with Nikon D3100	Minimum focus distance (m)	Filter size (mm)	Dimensions (diameter / length) (mm)	Weight (g)
DX LENSES						
10.5mm f/2.8G DX Fisheye	CRC	180°	0.14	Rear	63 x 62.5	300
10–24mm f/3.5–4.5G ED AF-S DX	ED, IF, SWM	109°–61°	0.24	77	82.5 x 87	460
12–24mm f/4G ED IF AF-S DX	SWM	99°–61°	0.3	77	82.5 x 90	485
16–85mm f/3.5–5.6G ED VR AF-S DX	VRII, SWM	83°–18.5°	0.38	67	72 x 85	485
17–55mm f/2.8G ED IF AF-S DX	ED, SWM	79°–28.5°	0.36	77	85.5 x 11.5	755
18–55mm f/3.5–5.6G AF-S VR DX	VR, SWM	76°–28.5°	0.28	52	73 x 79.5	265
18–55mm f/3.5–5.6GII AF-S DX	ED, SWM	76°–28.5°	0.28	52	70.5 x 74	205
18–70mm f/3.5–4.5G ED IF AF-S DX	ED, SWM	76°–22.5°	0.38	67	73 x 75.5	420
18–105mm f/3.5–5.6G ED VR AF-S DX	ED, IF, VRII, NC, SWM	76°–15.3°	0.45	67	76 x 89	420
18–135mm f/3.5–5.6 ED IF AF-S DX	ED, SWM	76°–12°	0.45	67	73.5 x 86.5	385
18–200mm f/3.5–5.6G ED AF-S VRII DX	ED, SWM, VRII	76°–8°	0.5	72	77 x 96.5	560
35mm f/1.8G AF-S	SWM	44°	0.3	52	70 x 52.5	210
55–200mm f/4–5.6 AF-S VR DX	ED, SWM, VR	28.5°–8°	1.1	52	73 x 99.5	335
55–200mm f/4–5.6G ED AF-S DX	ED, SWM	28.5°–8°	0.95	52	68 x 79	255
55–300mm f/4.5–5.6G ED VR	ED, SWM	28.5°–5.2°	1.4	58	76.5 x 123	530
85mm f/3.5G ED VR AF-S DX Micro Nikkor	ED, IF, SWM, VRII	18.5°	0.28	52	73 x 98.5	355

	Optical features / notes	Angle of view with Nikon D3100	Minimum focus distance (m)	Filter size (mm)	Dimensions (diameter / length) (mm)	Weight (g)
AF PRIME LENSES						
14mm f/2.8D ED AF	ED, RF	90°	0.2	Rear	87 x 86.5	670
16mm f/2.8D AF Fisheye	CRC	120°	0.25	Rear	63 x 57	290
20mm f/2.8D AF	CRC	70°	0.25	62	69 x 42.5	270
24mm f/1.4G ED	ED, NC	61°	0.25	77	83 x 88.5	620
24mm f/2.8D AF		61°	0.3	52	64.5 x 46	270
28mm f/2.8D AF		53°	0.25	52	65 x 44.5	205
35mm f/2D AF		44°	0.25	52	64.5 x 43.5	205
35mm f/1.4G AF-S	NC, SWM	44°	0.3	67	83 x 89.5	600
50mm f/1.8D AF		31.3°	0.45	52	63 x 39	160
50mm f/1.4D AF		31.3°	0.45	52	64.5 x 42.5	230
50mm f/1.4G AF-S	IF, SWM	31.3°	0.45	58	73.5 x 54	280
85mm f/1.4G AF	SWM, NC	18.5°	0.85	77	86.5 x 84	595
85mm f/1.8D AF	RF	18.5°	0.85	62	71.5 x 58.5	380
105mm f/2D AF DC	DC	15.2°	0.9	72	79 x 111	640
135mm f/2D AF DC	DC	12°	1.1	72	79 x 120	815
180mm f/2.8D ED IF AF	ED, IF	9.1°	1.5	72	78.5 x 144	760
200mm f/2G ED IF AF-S VRII	ED, VRII, SWM	8.2°	1.9	52	124 x 203	2930
300mm f/2.8G ED VR II AF-S	ED, VRII, NC, SWM	5.2°	2.2	52	124 x 267.5	2900
300mm f/4D ED IF AF-S	ED, IF	5.2°	1.45	77	90 x 222.5	1440
300mm f/2.8 ED IF AF-S VR	ED, SWM, NC	5.2°	2.2	52	124 x 268	2850
400mm f/2.8G ED VR AF-S	ED, IF, VRII, NC	4°	2.9	52	159.5 x 368	4620
400mm f/2.8D ED IF AF-S II	ED, SWM	4°	3.8	52	160 x 352	4800
500mm f/4G ED VR AF-S	IF, ED, VRII, NC	3.1°	4	52	139.5 x 391	3880
500mm f/4D ED IF AF-S II	ED, IF	3.1°	5	52	140 x 394	3800
600mm f/4G ED VR AF-S	ED, IF, VRII, NC	2.4°	5	52	166 x 445	5060
600mm f/4D ED IF AF-S II	ED, SWM	2.4°	6	52	166 x 445	5900

AF ZOOM LENSES

14–24mm f/2.8G ED AF-S	IF, ED, SWM, NC	90°–61°	0.28	None	98 x 131.5	970
16–35mm f/4G ED VR	NC, ED, VR	83°–44°	0.29	77	82.5 x 125	745
17–35mm f/2.8D ED IF AF-S	IF, ED, SWM	79°–44°	0.28	77	82.5 x 106	745
18–35mm f/3.5-4.5D ED	ED	76°–44°	0.33	77	82.7 x 82.5	370
24–70mm f/2.8G ED AF-S	ED, SWM, NC	61°–22.5°	0.38	77	83 x 133	900
24–85mm f/2.8–4D IF AF		61°–18.5°	0.5	72	78.5 x 82.5	545
24–120mm f/4G ED IF AF-S VR	ED, SWM, NC, VRII	61°–13.5°	0.45	77	84 x 103.5	710
28–70mm f/2.8 ED IF AF-S	ED, SWM	53°–22.5°	0.7	77	88.5 x 121.5	935
28–300mm f/3.5-5.6G ED VR	ED, SWM	53°–5.2°	0.5	77	83 x 114.5	800
70–200mm f/2.8G ED IF AF-S VRII	ED, SWM, VRII	22.5°–8°	1.4	77	87 x 209	1540
70–300mm f/4.5-5.6G AF-S VR	ED, IF, SWM, VRII	22.5°–5.20°	1.5	67	80 x 143.5	745
80–400mm f/4.5-5.6D ED VR AF	ED, VR	20°–4°	2.3	77	91 x 171	1340
200–400mm f/4G ED IF AF-S VRII	ED, NC, VRII, SWM	8°–4°	2	52	124 x 365.5	3360

MACRO LENSES

60mm f/2.8G ED AF-S Micro	ED, SWM, NC	26.3°	0.185	62	73 x 89	425
60mm f/2.8D AF Micro	CRC	26.3°	0.219	62	70 x 74.5	440
105mm f/2.8G AF-S VR Micro	ED, IF, VRII, NC, SWM	15°	0.31	62	83 x 116	720
200mm f/4D ED IF AF Micro	ED, CRC	8°	0.5	62	76 x 104.5	1190

PERSPECTIVE CONTROL

24mm f/3.5D ED PC-E (manual focus)	ED, NC	56°	0.21	77	82.5 x 108	730
45mm f/2.8D ED PC-E (manual focus)	ED, NC	34.5°	0.25	77	83.5 x 112	780
85mm f/2.8D ED PC-E (manual focus)	ED, NC	18.9°	0.39	77	82.7 x 107	65

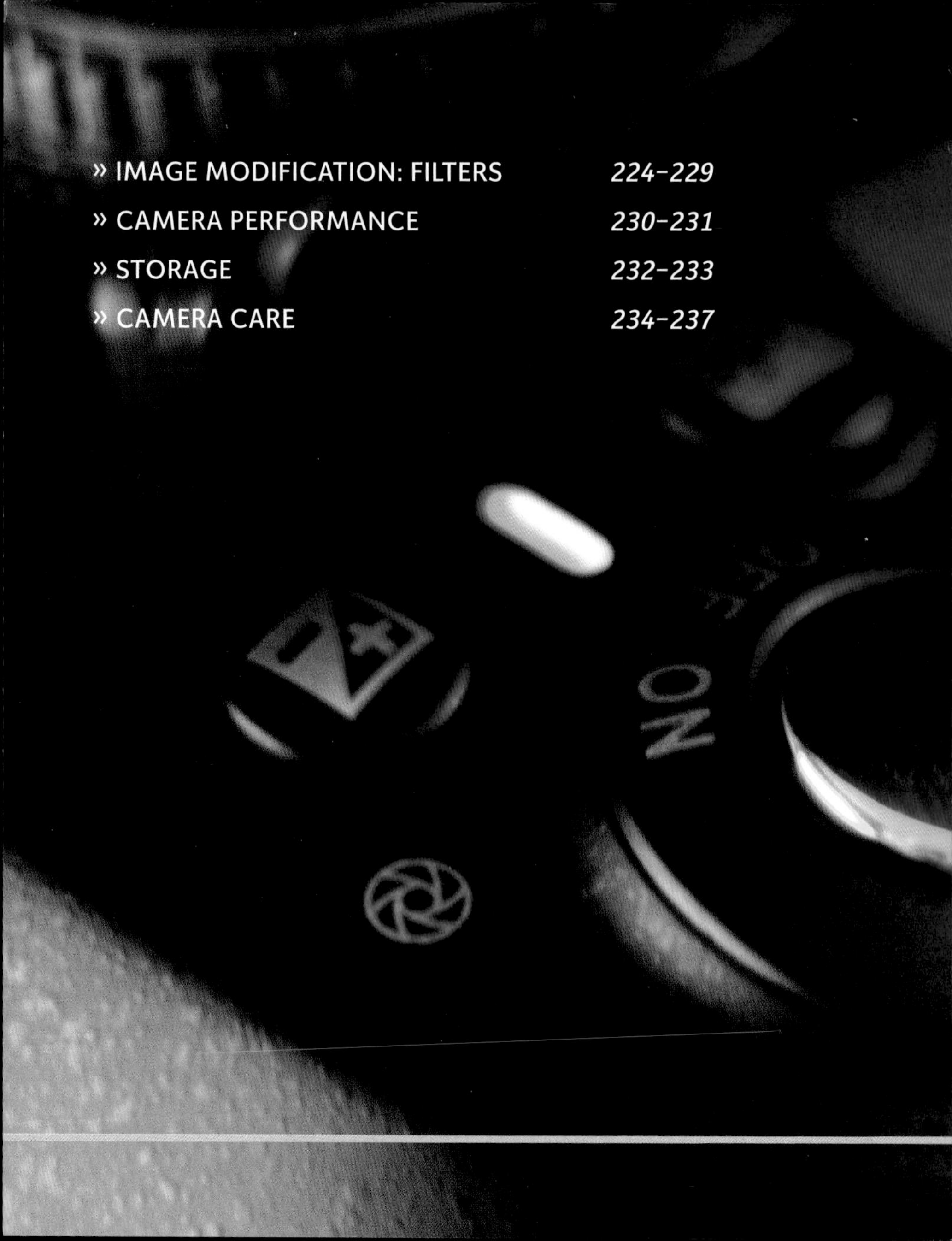
ON

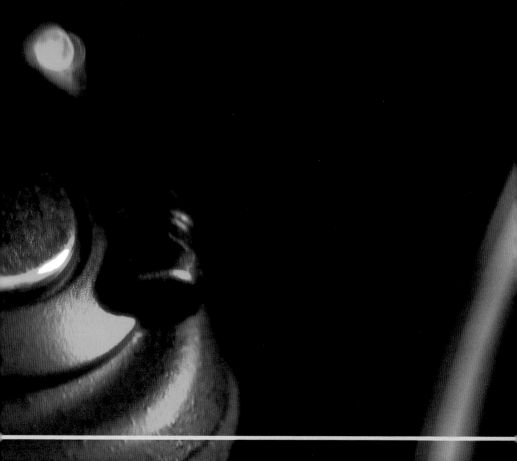

Chapter 8
ACCESSORIES & CAMERA CARE

8 ACCESSORIES

As part of the vast Nikon system, a wide choice of accessories is available for the D3100. In addition to Nikon's own products, there are many third-party items that further extend the range of options, with accessories grouped into four main types: image modification (filters and flash), camera performance, camera support, and storage.

» IMAGE MODIFICATION: FILTERS

Flash and close-up accessories have already been dealt with in preceding chapters, leaving filters for us to look at here. However, it's fair to say that some types of filter are almost redundant with digital cameras; variable white balance, for example, has all but eliminated the need for color-correction filters.

Therefore, the general advice for digital photography is to avoid using filters unnecessarily, as adding extra layers of glass in front of the lens can increase the risk of flare or otherwise degrade the image. "Stacking" multiple filters increases the risk, and heightens the chance of vignetting.

There is one exception to this rule, though, which is to keep a UV or skylight filter permanently attached to every lens you own—not to act as a filter as such, but as the first line of defence against knocks and scratches. Filters are much cheaper to replace than lenses.

Types of filter

There are three main classes of filters, defined by the way they attach to the lens: round, screw-in filters; slot-in filters; and rear or drop-in filters.

Round filters screw to the front of the lens and are normally made of high-quality optical glass. The filter-thread diameter (in mm) of most Nikon lenses is specified in the tables on pages 219-221, and usually marked around the front of the lens next to the Ø symbol. Nikon produces screw-in filters in sizes matching the range of Nikkor lenses and to the same high optical standards. Larger ranges come from Hoya, B+W, and other filter manufacturers.

Slot-in filters are more economical and convenient for those who use filters extensively. The filters—normally square or rectangular, and made of optical resin or gelatin—fit into a slotted holder, so with a simple adaptor ring for each lens you only need one filter holder and one set of filters to serve any number of lenses. The best-known maker is Cokin, although the Lee Filters range is widely used by more demanding users.

A few specialist lenses, such as super-telephotos with huge front elements, or extreme wide-angle and fish-eye lenses with protruding front elements, require equally specialist filters, either fitting to the rear of the lens, or dropping into a slot in the lens barrel. A few lenses, such as the 14–24mm f/2.8G ED AF-S Nikkor, make no provision for attaching filters.

UV and skylight filters

These filters are almost interchangeable, as both cut out the excess ultraviolet light that can make images appear excessively cool and blue, although a skylight filter also has a slight warming effect. As already suggested, the major benefit of both of these filters is to protect the front element of the lens.

UV FILTER FOR PROTECTION ⌄

A UV or skylight filter helps to protect the lens from spray, dust, dirt, and other hazards such as scratches.

ISO: 400 *Focal Length:* 52mm
Shutter Speed: 1/200 sec. *Aperture:* f/10

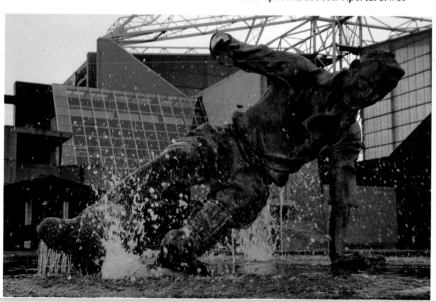

8 Polarizing filters

The polarizing filter, much loved by landscape photographers, cuts down reflections from most surfaces, intensifying the colors in rocks and vegetation, for example. It can also make reflections on water and glass virtually disappear, restoring transparency. This is most effective when the filter is at an angle of around 30 degrees to the surface. Rotating the filter in its mount strengthens or weakens its effect.

A polarizer can also cut through atmospheric haze (though not mist or fog) to make blue skies appear more intense. This effect is strongest when shooting at right angles to the direction of the sunlight and vanishes when the sun is directly behind or in front. Results can sometimes appear exaggerated, though, and with

wide-angle lenses it can be conspicuously uneven across the field of view. A polarizer should therefore be used with discrimination, and should certainly not be permanently attached to the lens. However, many of its effects cannot be fully replicated in any other way—even in digital post-processing—so while you may only use it occasionally, when you do, the result can be impossible to recreate in any other way.

Note:
Polarizing filters come in two types: linear and circular (though all polarizing filters are circular in shape). Only circular polarizers are suitable for the D3100.

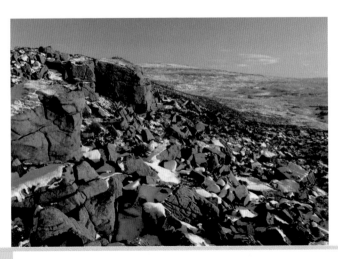

USING A POLARIZER »
TO BOOST COLOR
A polarizing filter has helped intensify the color in this shot, especially in the sky.

ISO: 1000
Focal Length: 24mm
Shutter Speed: 1/200 sec.
Aperture: f/9

Neutral density filters

Neutral density (ND) filters reduce the amount of light reaching the lens. "Neutral" simply means that they don't affect the color of the light, only its intensity. ND filters can be either plain or graduated.

A plain ND filter is useful when you want to set a slower shutter speed and/or wider aperture, but can't reduce the ISO setting any further. A classic example is when shooting waterfalls, where a long shutter speed is often favored to create a silky blur from the falling water. The strength of ND filters is specified on a scale where 0.3 represents a reduction of one full stop (1EV) of light, 0.6 is two stops (2EV), and so on.

Graduated ND filters have neutral density over half their area, with the other

Tip

If you're happy to invest some time at the computer you can often replicate—and even improve on—the effect of a graduated ND filter. It's particularly useful when the skyline is irregular; for example in mountainous areas, where the straight transition of an ND grad filter is unpleasantly obvious. The best way to selectively manipulate just part of an image is using Layer Masks, which gives complete control over the boundary between the areas affected. This may appear an advanced technique, but it soon becomes quick and intuitive. However, it can't work unless the original image captures detail in the highlights and shadows to start with.

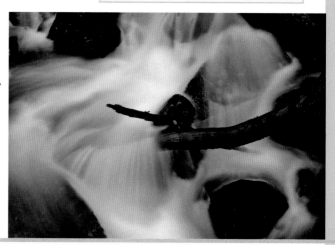

USING AN ND FILTER TO »
EXTEND THE EXPOSURE
A plain neutral density filter may be useful when you want to use really slow shutter-speeds.

ISO: 100
Focal Length: 70mm
Shutter Speed: 3 seconds (with bean bag)
Aperture: f/32

half being clear, and a gradual transition in the center. They are widely used in landscape photography to compensate for differences in brightness between the sky and land.

Special effects filters

Special effects filters come in many forms, but two common types are soft-focus filters and starburst filters. The soft-focus filter is widely used in portrait photography to soften skin blemishes, but its effects can be replicated and extended, precisely and reversibly, in digital post-processing.

Much the same is true of the starburst, and most other special-effects filters. There was a rash of such images in the 1970s when the Cokin system first became available to stills photographers, but most people soon tired of the more gimmicky effects, and such images still tend to look dated. It's usually better to capture the original image "straight," without filters, and apply effects later. That way you can always change your mind!

IN-CAMERA EFFECTS ⌄
The Red Intensifier effect in the Retouch menu.

ISO: 400 *Focal Length:* 70mm
Shutter Speed: 1/60 sec. *Aperture:* f/5.6

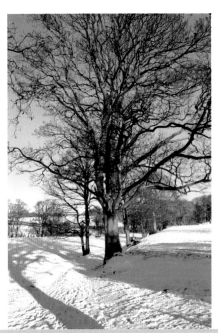

> ### Tip
>
> The **Filter effects** section of the D3100's Retouch menu, mimics the effects of several common photographic filters, including **Skylight** and **Warm**, while **Cross screen** offers a variety of "starburst" filter effects.

DUCKS BY RIVER WYRE, »
LANCASHIRE
There was a huge difference in brightness between the sky and foreground in this scene. A graduated filter offered a crude solution, but for a more subtle result two RAW conversions were combined using Layer Masks in Photoshop.

ISO: 200 *Focal Length:* 18mm
Shutter Speed: 1/8000 sec. *Aperture:* f/11

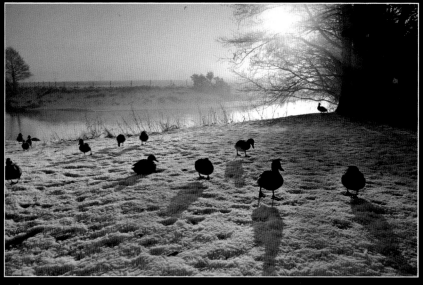

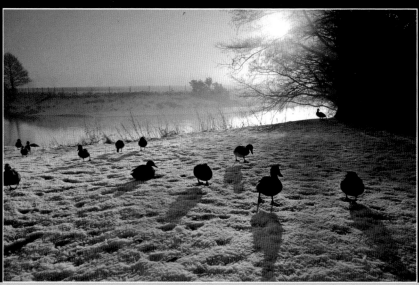

Numerous add-ons are available to improve or modify the performance of the D3100. Nikon includes several items in the box with the camera, but these are really essentials, not extras.

EN-EL14 battery

Without a battery, the D3100 is a dead-weight. While the camera is economical with batteries, it's always advisable to have a fully-charged spare on hand, especially if shooting in cold conditions.

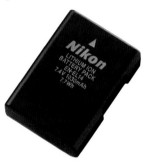

Tip

Nikon does not make a "booster" battery pack for the D3100, but third-party suppliers will probably soon do so. These attach to the base of the camera and typically allow two batteries to be used to double the shooting capacity.

MH-24 charger

Vital for keeping the EN-EL14 battery charged and ready.

BF-1A body cap

Keeps the interior of the camera free of dust and dirt when no lens is attached.

Video cable EG-D100

Required to connect the camera to a standard (not HD) television or video recorder (VCR).

› Optional extras

AC Adapter EH-5a/EH-5

Either of these adapters can be used to power the camera directly from the AC mains, allowing uninterrupted shooting in, for example, long studio sessions. (A Power Connector EP-5 is also required).

Remote Cords

Nikon's 1 meter-/3ft-long MC-DC2 remote cord can be used to remotely release the shutter without touching the camera. This can be used to help to minimize vibration.

GPS Unit GP-1

Nikon's dedicated Global Positioning System device.

Viewfinder lenses

The D3100's viewfinder has built-in dioptric adjustment, but if your eyesight is outside its range, Nikon produces a series of viewfinder lenses between −5 and +3 m^{-1}, with the designation DK-20C.

> **Tip**
>
> *It's usually easier to wear contact lenses or glasses than worry about supplementary viewfinder lenses. My prescription is around −5 m^{-1} and I've never had any problem using the D3100 while wearing contact lenses: simply set the built-in dioptric adjustment while wearing your usual glasses/lenses.*

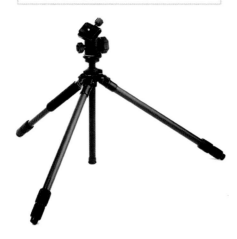

› Camera support

There's much more to camera support than tripods, although these remain a staple for most photographers.

Tripods

The D3100's ability to produce good-quality images at high ISO settings encourages handholding the camera, but there are still many occasions where a tripod is preferable. While light weight and low cost always appeal, beware of flimsy tripods that aren't sturdy enough to provide decent support, especially with longer lenses—a good tripod is an investment that should last many years. The best combination of low weight with rigidity comes in titanium or carbon fiber models, although these can cost as much as the camera, making aluminum the most popular option.

When shooting movies, a tripod is essential, and many tripods are designed specifically for this purpose.

> **Tip**
>
> *Many hikers will already be aware that some walking/trekking poles incorporate a camera-mount, so can double as a lightweight monopod.*

» STORAGE

Monopods

Monopods can't offer the same stability as a tripod, but they are lighter, easier to carry, and quicker to set up, which is why sports photographers who often have to react quickly while using heavy telephoto lenses favor them.

Other camera support

There are many other types of camera support, including both proprietary products and improvised alternatives. It's still hard to beat the humble beanbag, though, which can be homemade, or bought from various suppliers.

BEANBAG ❯❯
A simple, homemade beanbag that has served me well for many years.

Memory cards

The D3100 stores images on Secure Digital (SD), SDHC and SDXC cards. On long trips it's easy to fill up even large-capacity memory cards and as they are now remarkably cheap, it's advisable to carry a spare or two. Fast data-writing speeds can speed up the camera's operation.

Portable storage devices

Memory cards rarely fail, but that doesn't mean they *never* fail, so it's a good idea to back up valuable images as soon as possible. Many photographers use some sort of mobile device, and a dedicated photo storage unit such as the Vosonic VP8870 or Epson P-7000 combines a compact hard drive with a screen for reviewing and organizing your pictures. However, many of us already own something that will also store images, in the shape of an iPod. Not all iPod models are suitable, so investigate carefully. The iPad (but not the iPhone) also works well for this, but you will need a dedicated camera connector.

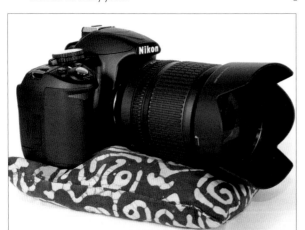

Card care

If a memory card is lost or damaged, your images are lost too. Blank cards are cheap, but cards full of images can be irreplaceable—unlike the camera itself. As SD cards use solid-state memory they are pretty robust, but it's still wise to treat them with care. Keep them in their original plastic cases, or something more robust, and avoid exposure to extremes of temperature, direct sunlight, liquids, and strong electromagnetic fields.

LONG EXPOSURES ⌄

Tripods are ideal for a wide variety of subjects.

ISO: 400 *Focal Length:* 50mm
Shutter Speed: 8 seconds (with tripod)
Aperture: f/8

> **Note:**
> *There seems to be no evidence that modern airport X-ray machines have any harmful effect on either digital cameras or memory cards.*

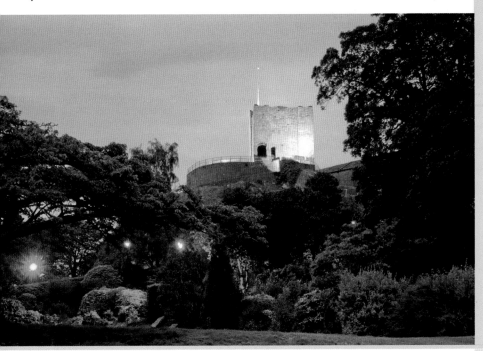

8 » CAMERA CARE

The Nikon D3100 is a solid, well-made camera, but it is still packed with highly complex electronic and optical technology, which can be vulnerable to damage. A few simple, common-sense precautions should ensure that it keeps functioning perfectly for many years.

› Basic care

Keeping the camera clean is a fundamental aspect of care. Removing dust and dirt with a blower, then wiping with a soft, dry cloth can clean the camera body. After exposure to salt spray, wipe off carefully with a cloth dampened with distilled water,

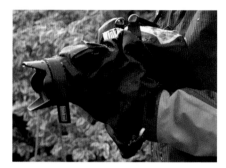

A very effective raincover; prevention ⌃ (protection) is better than cure.

then dry thoroughly. As prevention is better than cure, keep the camera in a case when not in use.

Lenses require special care, as glass elements and coatings are easily scratched, which this will degrade your images. Remove dust and dirt with a blower, while fingerprints and other marks should be removed using a dedicated lens cleaner and optical grade cloth. Again, prevention is better than cure, so the use of a skylight or UV filter to protect the lens is advisable, and lens caps should be replaced when the lens is not in use.

Warning!

The Nikon Reference manual (supplied on CD) seems to imply that the reflex mirror can be cleaned with a soft cloth and lens cleaning fluid. This goes against all advice from every other source, which is to **never touch the reflex mirror** *in any way. This is because its coating is very delicate, and the mirror itself can easily be misaligned, with dire consequences for viewing and focusing. Instead, remove dust from the mirror with the gentle use of an air-blower, taking great care during this process—and at all other times—***not** *to touch the mirror.*

› Screen care

The LCD monitor is central to the way that you interact with your camera, as most settings can only be viewed and changed there. It is also where you review the shots you've taken. While there's no need to touch the screen with your fingers, it does tend to come into contact with your nose when you're using the viewfinder. If you carry the camera round your neck, the screen will also bounce and swing against your clothes, so be aware of any buttons, zips, or other hard objects that could scratch the screen.

Nikon does not supply a screen protector with the D3100, but there are plenty of third-party suppliers who produce a variety of suitable screen protectors, and one of these would be a sound investment.

When the screen needs cleaning, use a blower to remove loose dirt, and then wipe the surface carefully with a clean, soft cloth. Do not apply pressure and do not use water or chemical cleaners.

Warning!

Never use household cleaning products anywhere near your camera.

Storage

If the camera is going to be left unused for an extended period of time, remove the battery, close the battery compartment cover, and store it in a cool dry place. Avoid extremes of temperature, high humidity, and strong electromagnetic fields such as those produced by television and computer equipment.

› Cleaning the sensor

To speak of sensor cleaning is slightly misleading as the sensor is protected by a low-pass filter. However, this can attract specks of dust and dirt, which will appear as dark spots or smears in your images and, unless you never change the lens, some dust will eventually find its way in.

Fortunately, the D3100 is well-equipped to keep dust at bay. Its Airflow control system helps to minimize the amount of dust settling in the first place, while its automated sensor cleaning will usually shift the majority of dust that does get in. These two measures greatly reduce the occurrence of dust spots and the resultant need for other forms of cleaning—earning heartfelt thanks from anyone who's experienced them!

Occasionally, however, stubborn spots may still appear on the low-pass filter, and it then becomes necessary to clean it by hand. This requires a clean, draught-free area with good light, preferably using a lamp that can be directed (from a safe distance) into the camera's interior. Some systems include magnifiers that allow close inspection of the low-pass filter, as well as dedicated cleaning swabs.

Make sure the battery is fully charged, or use a mains adaptor if you have one. Remove the lens, switch the camera **ON**, and select **Lock mirror up for cleaning** from the Setup menu. Press the shutter-release button to lock up the mirror and attempt to remove dust using a hand-blower (*not* compressed air or other aerosol). If this appears ineffective, consider using a dedicated sensor-cleaning swab, and carefully follow the instructions supplied with it. *Do not* use other brushes or cloths and never touch the low-pass filter with your finger. The filter is very delicate (and the sensor itself even more so). When cleaning is complete, turn the camera **OFF** and the mirror will reset.

Warning!

Any damage to the low-pass filter from incorrect use of a cleaning swab could void your warranty. If in doubt, consult a professional dealer or camera repairer.

Tip

If, despite your best efforts, spots continue to appear on your images, they can always be removed using the Clone *tool or* Healing brush *in* Adobe Photoshop. *In* Nikon Capture NX2 *this process can be automated by creating a* Dust-off *reference image. Spot-removal can be applied across batches of images in* Adobe Lightroom 3.

› Coping with cold

Nikon specify an operating temperature range for the D3100 of 32-104°F (0-40°C). This does not mean that the camera cannot be used when the temperature is below freezing, but the camera should be kept within the stated range if possible. Keeping the camera in an insulated case or under outer layers of clothing between shots will help to keep it warmer than the surroundings, but don't put it too near your skin as condensation can become a problem. If it does become cold, battery life may be severely reduced and, in extreme cold, the LCD display may become erratic or disappear completely. Ultimately, the camera may stop working altogether, but if allowed to warm up gently, this should not result in any permanent damage.

› Heat and humidity

Extremes of heat, and especially humidity (Nikon stipulate over 85%), can be even more problematic than extremes of cold, and are more likely to lead to long-term damage. In particular, rapid transfers from cool environments (say, an aircraft cabin) to hot and humid ones (the streets of Bangkok) can lead to condensation within the lens and camera. Before such a transition is anticipated, pack the camera and lens(es) in airtight containers with sachets of silica gel, which absorbs moisture. Allow the equipment to reach the ambient temperature before unpacking and using it.

› Water protection

The D3100 does not claim to be waterproof, but brief exposure to light rain is unlikely to do permanent harm. Exposure should be minimized, however, and the camera wiped regularly with a microfiber cloth: a cloth of this kind is always handy to wipe off any accidental splashes. Avoid using the built-in flash if it's raining or the camera is likely to be splashed, and try to keep the hotshoe cover in place to help prevent water reaching the electronic flash contacts. Double-check that all access covers on the camera are properly closed.

Salt water is particularly hostile to electronic components, so take extra care to avoid any contact. If this does occur, clean the camera carefully and immediately with a cloth lightly dampened with fresh water—preferably distilled/deionized water.

Better still, in wet conditions, protect the camera with a waterproof cover when you're out—a simple plastic bag will provide reasonable protection, but purpose-made rain-guards are available. Specialist waterproof cases provide complete protection from water, even allowing you to submerge the camera.

› Dust protection

To minimize the ingress of dust into the camera, take great care when changing lenses. Aim the camera slightly downward and stand with your back to any wind. In really bad conditions (such as sandstorms) it's best not to change lenses at all, and to protect the camera with a waterproof (and therefore dustproof) case. Dust that settles on the outside of the camera is relatively easy to remove; the safest way is with a hand-operated or compressed-air blower. Do this before changing lenses, memory cards, or batteries.

› Camera cases

No matter what the conditions, some sort of case is highly advisable to protect the camera when not in use. The most practical is a simple drop-in pouch that can be worn on a waist-belt: excellent examples come from makers such as Think Tank Photo, Camera Care Systems (CCS), and Lowepro.

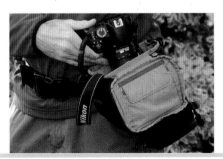

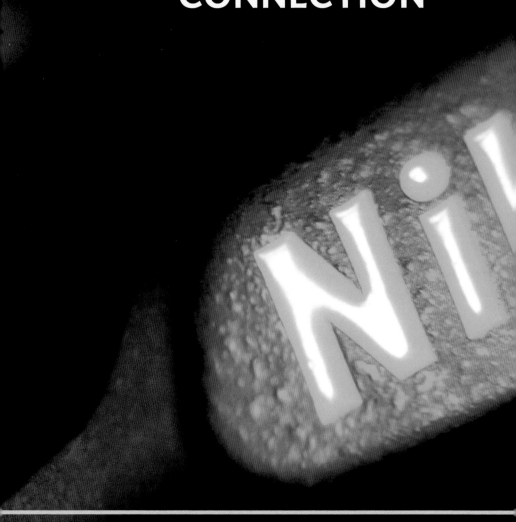

Chapter 9
CONNECTION

CONNECTION

Connecting to external devices—especially computers—is not an extension of digital photography: it's an essential part of the process, enabling you to store, organize, view, and print your images. The D3100 is designed to facilitate these operations out of the box, and all the main cables that are required are included with the camera.

The supplied EG-D2 cable is used to connect the camera to a normal television or VCR, but you can also connect the camera to a HDMI (High Definition Multimedia Interface) TV with an (optional) HDMI cable: the process is the same.

1) Check that the camera is set to the correct mode in the Setup menu (PAL or NTSC for standard televisions and VCRs, or HDMI).

2) Turn the camera off (it is important to do this before the cable is connected or disconnected from the camera).

3) Open the cover on the left side of the camera and insert the cable into the appropriate slot (A/V-out or HDMI).

4) Tune the television to its Video or HDMI channel.

5) Turn the camera **ON** and press the playback button. Images remain visible on the camera monitor as well as on the television screen and you navigate using the multi-selector in the usual way. The D3100's **Slide show** facility can be used to automate playback.

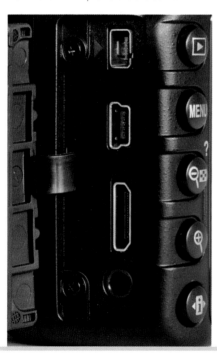

CONNECTION PORTS   **«**
Connection ports on the left side of the D3100.

» CONNECTING TO A PRINTER

The most flexible and powerful way to print photographs from the D3100 is to transfer them to a computer. This is the only option where RAW files are concerned, although you can always create JPEG copies in-camera.

The memory card can also be inserted into a compatible printer or taken to a photo printing outlet, or you can connect the camera to any printer that supports the PictBridge standard, allowing JPEG images to be printed directly.

To connect to a printer:
1) Turn the camera **OFF**.

2) Turn the printer **ON** and connect the supplied USB cable. Open the cover on the left side of the camera and insert the cable into the USB slot; the smaller end of the cable connects to the camera.

3) Turn the camera **ON**. You should now see a welcome screen, followed by a PictBridge playback display. There's now a choice between **Printing pictures one at a time** or **Printing multiple pictures**.

Image cropping
If **Crop** is selected, the image is displayed with a border delineating the crop area. Use the ⊖ and ⊕ buttons to change the size of the crop area and use the multi-

OPTIONS NAME	OPTIONS AVAILABLE	NOTES
Page size	Printer default 3.5 x 5 inches 5 x 7 inches A4	Options will be limited by the maximum size the printer can print.
No. of copies	1–99	Use ▲ / ▼ to choose the number of copies you wish to make, and then press ⊙ to select.
Border	Printer default Print with border No border	If Print with border is selected, the borders will be white.
Time stamp	Printer default Print time stamp No time stamp	Prints the time and date when the image was taken.
Crop	Crop No cropping	Prints selected area only to the size selected under Page size.

selector to reposition it if you don't want it centered. (This is similar to using **Trim** in the Retouch menu). When you are satisfied with the crop, press (OK).

Printing pictures one at a time

This process is very straightforward, particularly if you are already familiar with navigating the D3100's playback screens.

1) If the photo displayed is the one you wish to print, press (OK). This brings up a menu of printing options as shown on the previous page. Use the multi-selector to navigate through the menu and highlight specific options; press (OK) to select the highlighted option.

2) When the required options have been set, select **Start printing** and press (OK). To cancel at any time, press (OK) again.

Printing multiple pictures

The D3100 allows you to print several pictures at once, or create an index print of all the JPEG images that are currently stored on the memory card (up to 256 images). With the PictBridge menu displayed, press **MENU** and the options shown below are displayed.

Print Select	Use the multi-selector to scroll through the pictures on the memory card (displayed as 6 thumbnails at a time). To see an image full-screen, press ⊕. To choose the currently selected image for printing, hold **?** and press ▲. The picture is marked with a 🖴 and the number of prints is set to 1. Keep the **?** button depressed and use ▲ to change the number of prints. Repeat the above to select further images and choose the number of prints required from each. Finally, press (OK) to display the PictBridge menu and select printing options. *Note:* Only the options for Page size, Border, and Time stamp will be available. Select Start printing and press (OK).
Select Date	Print one copy of each image taken on a selected date.
Date (DPOF)	Prints images already selected using the Print set (DPOF) option in the Playback menu.
Index Print	Prints all JPEG images (up to a maximum of 256) on the memory card. If more than 256 images exist, only the first 256 will be printed. Options for Page size, Border and Time stamp can be set as already described. If the selected page size is too small for the number of images, a warning will be displayed.

» CONNECTING TO A COMPUTER

Connecting to a Mac or Windows PC allows you to store and backup your images. It also helps you exploit the power of the D3100 more fully, including the ability to optimize the image quality from RAW files. The supplied *Nikon Transfer* software allows you to control this process, while *Nikon View NX2* has a range of image-enhancement tools. *Nikon Capture NX2* (an optional extra) has greater capabilities, especially when working with RAW files.

Computer requirements

Most modern computers are more than capable of handling the D3100's still image and video files, although you will need a USB port for connecting the camera (or card reader), unless you connect wirelessly using an Eye-Fi card. You can install the

> **Note:**
> The supplied USB cable allows direct connection to a computer. However, it is often more convenient to transfer photos by inserting the memory card into a card-reader. Many PCs have built-in SD card slots but separate card readers are cheap and widely available. Older card readers may not support SDHC or SDXC cards.

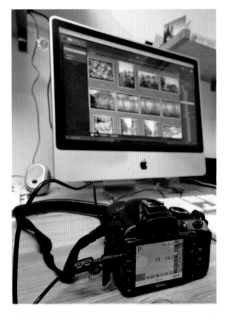

CONNECTED ⌃
A D3100 connected to a computer

CARD READER ⌄

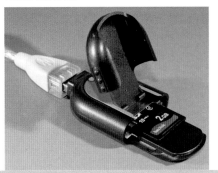

appropriate Nikon software from the CD supplied with the camera, or download it from the Nikon website.

Nikon Transfer and *Nikon View NX2* require one of the following operating systems: *Mac OS X* (Version 10.4.11 or later), *Windows 7*, *Windows Vista* with *Service Pack 2*, or *Windows XP* with *Service Pack 3*.

Mac OS 9 and earlier versions of Windows are not supported, although older computers will still be able to transfer and view images using third-party software. However, these systems may run very slowly when dealing with the large images generated by the D3100, and may have particular difficulty opening RAW files.

Tip

If your computer runs slowly when working with large image files, the most likely cause is insufficient memory (RAM). RAM can usually be added relatively easily and at a low cost. A shortage of free space on the hard disk may also cause your computer to run slowly.

Backing up

Until they are backed up, your images exist solely as data on the camera's memory card. Memory cards are robust, but not indestructible, and in any case you will surely wish to format and reuse them. However, when images are transferred to the computer and the card is formatted, those images still exist in one single location: the computer's hard drive. If anything happens to that hard drive—whether it's fire, theft, or hardware failure—you could lose thousands of irreplaceable images.

The simplest form of backup is a second, external hard drive that you connect to your computer using USB or FireWire. These are now very cheap to buy and most operating systems include automated system backup software that will not only copy your pictures and videos to your backup drive, but also your system programs, applications, and other data stored on your main hard disk.

BACKUP ≫
Time Machine maintains backups automatically.

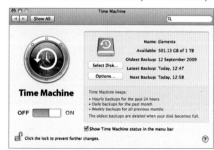

› Color calibration

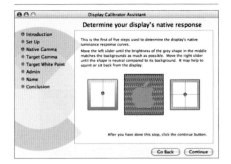

A major problem for digital camera users is that the color of images can seem to change its appearance, so what looked great on the camera's LCD screen can look different on the computer monitor, different again when you email them to your friends, and different still when printed. To achieve consistency across multiple devices, it's vital that your main computer monitor is correctly set up and calibrated. This may seem complex and time-consuming, but ultimately it saves a lot of time and frustration trying to constantly change the colors of your images. Detailed advice is beyond the scope of this book but there's more detail in the *DSLR Handbook* (from this author and publisher) and useful online advice at *www.cambridgeincolor.com/ tutorials.htm.*

› Connecting the camera

The following assumes that you have installed *Nikon Transfer* from the CD supplied with the camera, although you may prefer to use *Nikon View NX2, Nikon Capture NX,* or third-party software such as *iPhoto* to import your images. The procedure with other software is similar in outline, but different in detail: consult its manual or Help menu.

1) Turn the computer **ON** and allow it to start up fully. Open the cover on the left side of the camera and insert the smaller end of the supplied USB cable into the USB slot; insert the other end into a USB port on the computer (don't try connecting to unpowered USB hubs or ports on the keyboard; they won't work).

2) Turn the camera **ON**. *Nikon Transfer* starts automatically (unless you have configured its Preferences otherwise), and the window shown below appears.

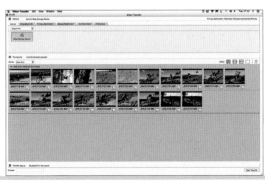

3) The *Nikon Transfer* window offers various options; for full detail see the Help menu in *Nikon Transfer* itself. The following are among the most important.

4) To transfer selected images only, use the **check box** below each thumbnail to select/deselect as required.

5) Click the **Primary Destination** tab to choose where your photographs will be stored. You can create a new subfolder for each transfer, rename images as they are transferred, and so on.

6) Click the **Backup Destination** tab if you want *Nikon Transfer* to create backup copies automatically during transfer.

Disconnecting the camera

Switch **OFF** the camera when transfer is complete, and disconnect the cable. *Nikon Transfer* will close automatically.
If you transfer your images using a card-reader, you must remove the card from the system in the same way as any other external drive: in *Windows* use **Safely**

> ### Tip
>
> *Always switch the camera* **OFF** *before connecting or disconnecting USB or other interface cables.*

Remove Hardware, and in *Mac OS X* use **Command+E** or drag the memory card's icon to the Trash.

Wireless connection (Eye-Fi)

Eye-Fi looks and operates like a conventional (albeit more expensive) SD memory card, but includes an antenna that enables it to connect to Wi-Fi networks, allowing the rapid transfer of images to a computer without cables.

Eye-Fi cards are supplied with a card reader, and when the card and reader are plugged into any recent Mac or PC the supplied software should install automatically (the computer must also have a Wi-Fi connection). There is then an automatic registration process that makes that computer the default destination for all Eye-Fi uploads. You can select a destination folder on your computer where you would like files to be transferred to, and you can also configure the system to automatically upload photos to sharing sites such as Flickr.

Once the configuration is complete, insert the card into the camera and select **Eye-Fi Upload** from the Setup menu. The camera will automatically upload images as they are taken, as long as you remain within signal range of the network. The D3100 displays a notification when images are being uploaded.

» NIKON SOFTWARE

The D3100 is bundled with *Nikon Transfer* and *Nikon View NX2* software. *Nikon Transfer* is a simple application that does one job well enough—transfering images from the camera to the computer.

Nikon View NX2 is a broader package that covers many of the main functions that digital photographers require, not only allowing you to transfer images, but to view them individually or browse through them, save them in different formats, and print them. Although *View NX2* is much better than *View NX*, editing and enhancing images (including RAW files) is still limited, slow, and it is not very intuitive, comparing poorly with applications such as Apple's *iPhoto*.

Nikon Capture NX2 has much greater functionality in that respect, but it comes at a premium price, and some may find it feels "awkward" compared to mainstream applications such as *Adobe Photoshop*.

Using Nikon View NX2

1) From a browser view such as the thumbnail grid (choose view mode from the **View** menu), click on a RAW image to highlight it. **Image Viewer** shows the image in more detail, plus a histogram, while **Full Screen** allows you to see the image full size.

2) Panels at the right side of the screen reveal **Metadata** and the **Adjustment** palette, which allows a range of adjustments to be made to the exposure, white balance, and so on. It also has access to Nikon Picture Controls.

3) Click away from the image and you will be asked if you want to save any adjustments. You do not need to export or convert the file immediately.

4) To export the file as a TIFF or JPEG that can be viewed, edited, and printed by most other applications, choose **Convert Files** from the **File** menu. Here you can set a new size for the image if required, and also change its name.

5) The **File Format** menu in the **Convert Files** dialog offers three options: **JPEG, TIFF (8-Bit)**, and **TIFF (16-Bit)** as detailed on the following page.

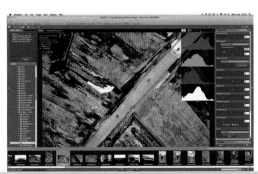

NIKON VIEW NX2 CONVERT FILES OPTIONS

JPEG	Highest Quality High Quality Good Balance Good Compression Ratio Highest Compression Ratio	Suitable if further (extensive) editing is not envisaged. Of the five options, Highest Quality is recommended unless storage space is at a premium, or the image is specifically intended for Website use or as an e-mail attachment.
TIFF(8-Bit)		Creates larger file sizes than JPEG but is a better choice if subsequent editing is envisaged.
TIFF(16-Bit)		The best choice when extensive retouching is anticipated. Images can be converted to 8-bit after editing, halving file size.

Nikon Capture NX2

Nikon Capture NX2 is a far more complete editing package when compared to *Nikon View* and for access to a full range of editing options, especially in relation to RAW files, *Nikon Capture NX2* (or a third-party alternative) is essential.

However, unlike rivals such as *Adobe Photoshop, Capture NX2* cannot open RAW files from non-Nikon cameras. *Photoshop* also has a much wider feature set, although this is perhaps to be expected: *Photoshop* costs almost four times as much as *Nikon Capture NX2*.

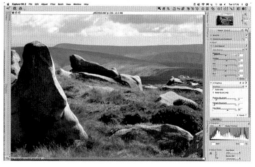

» THIRD-PARTY SOFTWARE

The undisputed industry standard image-editing program is *Adobe Photoshop*, the current version being *Photoshop CS5*. Its power is enormous and it is the subject of many dedicated books and websites. However, it perhaps offers far more than most users need, and many may prefer the more affordable *Photoshop Elements*, which has similarly sophisticated editing features, including the ability to open RAW files from the D3100.

Photoshop Elements also includes something that *Adobe Photoshop* itself does not; the *Organizer*. This allows photos to be sorted into Albums and "tagged" in different ways, and some sort of organizer or cataloging software soon becomes essential as you collect hundreds and then thousands of images.

Mac users have another excellent choice in the form of *iPhoto*, which is pre-loaded on all new Macs. Like *Photoshop Elements*, it combines organizing and editing, while Apple's elegant and intuitive interface makes it easy to get to grips with. The *Adjust* palette provides quick and flexible image editing, although—unlike *Photoshop Elements*—it cannot edit in 16-bit depth, which is recommended for best results.

Finally, for those who regularly use the RAW format, there are two one-stop

Note:
Older versions of **Adobe Photoshop** *will not recognize RAW files created by the D3100. These require the* **Camera Raw** *plug-in, version 6.3, which is incompatible with versions before* **Photoshop CS5.** *To work around this, without a costly upgrade, the free* **Adobe DNG Converter** *can be used to convert the D3100's RAW files into the "universal" DNG format. These can then be opened with older versions of* **Photoshop,** *and many other editing programs. Similar limitations apply to older versions of* **Photoshop Elements,** *but an upgrade here is less costly.*

solutions in the shape of Apple's *Aperture* (Mac only) and Adobe's *Lightroom* (Mac and PC). Both applications combine powerful organizing and cataloging tools with sophisticated and non-destructive image editing. Essentially this means that any changes you make to your image—including color, density, cropping, and so on—are recorded alongside the original RAW file without any need to create a new TIFF or JPEG file. TIFF or JPEG versions, incorporating all the edits, can be exported as and when needed.

» GLOSSARY

8-bit, 12-bit, 16-bit: *see* bit depth

Accessory shoe *see* hotshoe

Angle of view The lens opening that admits light. Relative aperture sizes are expressed as f-numbers or f-stops.

Aperture The opening in a camera lens through which light passes to expose the sensor. The relative size of the aperture is denoted by *f-stops*.

Artifact Occurs when data is interpreted incorrectly, resulting in visible flaws in an image.

Bit depth The amount of information recorded for each color channel. 8-bit, for example, means that the data distinguishes 256 levels of brightness for each channel. 16-bit images recognize over 65,000 levels per channel, which allows greater freedom in editing. The D3100 records RAW images with a 12-bit depth, which are converted to 16-bit when imported into the computer.

Bracketing Taking a number of otherwise identical shots in which just one parameter (i.e. exposure) is varied.

Buffer On-board memory that holds images until they can be written to the memory card.

Burst A number of frames shot in quick succession; the maximum burst size is limited by the camera's buffer capacity.

Channel The D3100, like other digital devices, records data for three separate color channels (*see* RGB).

CCD Charge-coupled device; a type of imaging sensor used in some digital cameras.

Clipping Complete loss of detail in highlight or shadow areas of the image (sometimes both), leaving them as pure white or pure black.

CMOS Complementary Metal Oxide Semiconductor; a type of image sensor used in some digital cameras, including the D3100.

Color temperature The color of light, expressed in degrees Kelvin (K). Confusingly, "cool" (bluer) light has a higher color temperature than "warm" (red) light.

CPU Central Processing Unit; a small computer in the camera (also found in many lenses) that controls most, or all, of the unit's functions.

Crop factor *see* focal length multiplication factor

Diopter Unit expressing the power of a lens.

dpi (dots per inch) A measure of resolution: should strictly be applied only to printers. *See also* ppi.

Dynamic range The range of brightness from shadows to highlights within which the camera can record detail.

Exposure Used in several senses. For instance, "an exposure" is virtually synonymous with "an image" or "a photograph": to make an exposure means to take a picture. Exposure also refers to the amount of light hitting the image sensor, and to systems for measuring this. *See also* overexposure, underexposure.

EV Exposure Value; a standardized unit of exposure. 1EV is equivalent to one "stop" in traditional photographic parlance, which may be one stop applied to the shutter speed, aperture, or ISO.

Extension rings/Extension tubes Hollow tubes that fit between the camera body and lens to allow greater magnifications.

f-number Also referred to as f-stop, relates to the lens aperture expressed as a fraction of focal length; f/2 is a wide aperture and f/16 is a small aperture.

Fast (lens) Lens with a wide maximum aperture, such as f/1.8. An aperture of f/4 might be considered relatively fast for long telephoto lenses.

Fill-in flash Flash used in combination with daylight. Used with naturally backlit or harshly side-lit subjects to prevent dark shadows.

Filter A piece of glass or plastic placed in front of, within, or behind the lens to modify the light passing through it.

Firmware Software that controls the camera: upgrades are issued by Nikon from time to time and can be transferred to the camera via a memory card.

Focal length The distance (in mm) from the optical center of a lens to the point at which light is focused.

Focal length multiplication factor
Because the D3100's sensor is smaller than a frame of 35mm film, the effective focal length of all lenses is multiplied by 1.5 to give a 35mm or "full-frame" equivalent.

fps (frames per second) The number of exposures (photographs) that can be taken in a second. The D3100's maximum frame rate is 3 fps.

Highlights The brightest areas of the scene and/or the image.

Histogram A graph representing the distribution of tones in an image, ranging from pure black to pure white.

Incident light metering Measuring the light falling on to a subject, usually with a separate meter. An alternative to the in-camera meter, which measures reflected light.

ISO International Standards Organisation. ISO ratings express film speed; the sensitivity of digital sensors is quoted as ISO-equivalent.

JPEG (Joint Photographic Experts Group) A compressed image file standard. High levels of JPEG compression can reduce files to about 5% of their original size, but there may be some loss of quality.

LCD Liquid crystal display; flat screen as used for the D3100's rear monitor.

Macro A term used to describe close focusing and the close-focusing ability of a lens. A true macro lens has a reproduction ratio of 1:1 or better.

Megapixel *see* pixel

Memory card A removable storage device for digital cameras.

Noise Image interference manifested as random variations in pixel brightness and/or color.

Overexposure When too much light reaches the sensor, resulting in an overly bright image, often with clipped highlights.

Pixel Picture element; the individual colored dots (usually square) that make up a digital image. One million pixels = 1 megapixel.

ppi Pixels per inch: should be applied to digital files rather than the commonly used dpi.

Reproduction ratio The ratio between the real size of an object and the size of its image on the sensor.

Resolution The number of pixels for a given dimension: for example, 300 pixels per inch. Resolution is often confused with image size. The native size of an image from the D3100 is 4608 x 3072 pixels, which could make a large (but coarse) print at 100 dpi or a smaller, but finer one at 300 dpi.

RGB Red Green Blue. Digital devices, including the D3100, record color in terms of brightness levels of the three primary colors.

Sensor The light-sensitive chip at the heart of every digital camera.

Shutter The mechanism that controls the amount of light reaching the sensor by opening and closing to expose the sensor when the shutter release button is pushed.

Speedlight Nikon's range of dedicated external flashguns.

Spot metering A metering system that takes its reading from the light reflected from a small portion of the scene.

Telephoto lens A lens with a large focal length and a narrow angle of view.

TIFF (Tagged image File Format) A universal file format supported by virtually all image-editing applications.

TTL Through The Lens, as used to describe the viewfinder and metering systems of SLR cameras such as the D3100.

Underexposure When insufficient light reaches the sensor, resulting in an overly dark image, often with clipped shadows.

USB (Universal Serial Bus) A data transfer standard, used to connect to a computer.

Viewfinder An optical system used for framing the image; on an SLR camera such as the D3100 it shows the view as seen through the lens.

White balance A function that compensates for different color temperatures so that images may be recorded with the correct color balance.

Wide-angle lens A lens with a short focal length and a wide angle of view.

Zoom A lens with a variable focal length, giving a range of viewing angles. To zoom in is to change focal length to give a narrower view and to zoom out is the converse. Optical zoom refers to the genuine zoom ability of a lens; digital zoom is the cropping of part of an image to produce an illusion of the same effect.

» USEFUL WEB SITES

NIKON-RELATED SITES

Nikon Worldwide
Home page for the Nikon Corporation
www.nikon.com

Nikon UK
Home page for Nikon UK
www.nikon.co.uk

Nikon USA
Home page for Nikon USA
www.nikonusa.com

Nikon User Support
European Technical Support Gateway
www.europe-nikon.com/support

Nikon Historical Society
Worldwide site for study of Nikon products
www.nikonhs.org

Nikon Links
Links to many Nikon-related sites
www.nikonlinks.com

Grays of Westminster
Revered Nikon-only dealer (London)
www.graysofwestminster.co.uk

GENERAL

Digital Photography Review
Independent news and reviews
www.dpreview.com

Thom Hogan
Real-world reviews and advice
www.bythom.com/nikon.htm

Jon Sparks
Landscape and outdoor pursuits
photography
www.jon-sparks.co.uk

EQUIPMENT

Adobe
Photoshop, Photoshop Elements, Lightroom
www.adobe.com/uk

Apple
Aperture and iPhoto
www.apple.com/uk/mac/

Aquapac
Waterproof cases
www.aquapac.net

Think Tank Photo
(Bags, holsters, rain-covers)
www.thinktankphoto.com

Sigma
Independent lenses and flash units
www.sigma-imaging-uk.com

PHOTOGRAPHY PUBLICATIONS

Ammonite Press
Photography books
www.ammonitepress.com

**Black & White Photography magazine,
Outdoor Photography magazine**
www.thegmcgroup.com

» INDEX